A Trip to Pike's Peak
& Notes Along the Way

BEING DESCRIPTIVE OF INCIDENTS AND
ACCIDENTS THAT ATTENDED THE PILGRIMAGE OF
THE COUNTRY THROUGH KANSAS AND NEBRASKA;
ROCKY MOUNTAINS; MINING REGIONS; MINING
OPERATIONS, Etc., Etc.

By

C. M. CLARK, M. D.

Edited by P. David & Jan Smith

Originally Published in Chicago, 1861

Revised Edition

WESTERN REFLECTIONS PUBLISHING COMPANY®
Lake City, Colorado

All rights reserved in whole or in part.
ISBN 978-1-932738-79-7

First Edition
Printed in the United States of America

Cover Design by Angela P. Hollingsworth
APH creative design, Lake City, CO

Copyright © Western Reflections Publishing Co.
951 N. Highway 149
P. O. Box 1149
Lake City, CO 81235
800-993-4490
970- 944-0110
publisher@westernreflectionspublishing.com
www.westernreflectionspublishing.com

PREFACE

The presence of gold in the Rocky Mountains had been the subject of rumors in the United States since the Mexican-American War and the gold rush to California. It was also known that the Spanish had for centuries looked for gold and silver in the mountains of present-day Colorado. As early as 1849, small amounts of gold were found by travelers going to California. After this time some Native Americans from the Rocky Mountains became aware of the value of gold to the white man and would occasionally show up with gold nuggets to trade for provisions.

A few Americans found small amounts of gold in the area between Long's Peak and Pike's Peak in 1857, and in the spring of 1858 William Green Russell led the first organized party of gold seekers (which included two of his brothers) into what would become Colorado Territory. The Russells were from Georgia (an area of the country where gold had been found in small quantities), but they tied in with a party of Cherokees from Oklahoma Indian Territory and a small number of men from Missouri before finishing their trip across the plains. By the time the group reached Cherry Creek, at the edge of the mountains, there were about 100 men in the party.

By mid-summer of 1858, many of the prospectors had given up and gone home discouraged because they were only finding small amounts of gold flakes instead of the large gold nuggets that had been found in California. But those few men who stayed to prospect pushed further west into the mountains, from present-day Wyoming all the way south to Pikes Peak, and a few even went as far south as New Mexico. The relatively small amount of gold that they brought back to Leavenworth and Kansas City in the late summer and early fall of 1858 produced a considerable amount of excitement – even though the gold had only been gained by long and tedious labor and no large amount of gold had been found at any one spot. By late summer, rumors of large gold strikes were being spread up and down the Missouri and Mississippi Rivers. Much of the United States was still suffering from the financial panic of 1857, and many men were desperate to again see financial prosperity. The prospect of discovering gold, and thereby instantly solving their financial problems, was very enticing.

Although the early prospectors encouraged men to wait until the next spring, some people started out immediately for the mountains, and there were soon quite a few parties building cabins around the South Platte River and Cherry Creek. A town even started to take shape under the name of Auraria. Many of these men traveled into the mountains and panned for gold in the middle of the winter, and they did fairly well – some even panning four to ten dollars of gold a day at a time when three to four dollars was considered a fair day's wage.

George A. Jackson found the first gold nuggets in Clear Creek on January 7, 1859, but it was spring before any real prospecting could be done. Badly inflated reports on the amount of gold being found filtered back to the States. Soon outright lies were being spread that gold nuggets could be picked up everywhere by just keeping your eyes on the ground. Newspaper articles and guidebooks all declared the new rallying cry - "Pikes Peaks or Bust." Ox wagons, mule trains, and men on foot were on their way. The "Rush to the Rockies" had started.

Preface

As the *Missouri Republican* of March 10, 1859 put it:

> Pike's Peak is in everybody's mouth and thoughts, and Pike's Peak figures in a million dreams. Every clothing store is a depot for outfits for Pike's Peak. There are Pike's Peak hats, and Pike's Peak guns, Pike's Peak boots, Pike's Peak shovels, and Pike's Peak goodness-knows-what-all, designed expressly for the use of emigrants and miners.... We presume that there are, or will be, Pike's Peak pills, manufactured with exclusive reference to the diseases of Cherry Creek Valley, and sold in connection with Pike's Peak guide books; or Pike's Peak schnapps to give tone to the stomachs of overtasked gold diggers; or Pike's Peak goggles to keep the gold dust out of the eyes of the fortune hunters; or Pike's Peak steelyards (drawing fifty pounds) with which to weigh the massive chunks of gold quarried out of Mother Earth's prolific bowels.

Soon, scores of men were arriving at the gold fields daily. Most had no idea how or where to find gold. Many were so poorly supplied for the trip that they had to turn back before reaching the Rockies or they would have starved to death. But more and more men, many accompanied by their entire families, kept coming. On May 6, 1859, near present-day Black Hawk and Central City, John H. Gregory discovered the first gold vein from which gold "float" was being found in the river. What came to be known as Jackson's Diggings and Gregory's Gulch were soon filled with men.

In early June, 1859, William Green Russell (spelled "Russel" by Clark) found a considerable amount of gold (six men found seventy-six ounces [worth $16 to $20 per ounce] in one week), and claims were filed all over the gulch that soon bore his name. A second stampede of men occurred in 1860, despite the fact that only limited discoveries were being made and the districts had become extremely overcrowded.

The author of this book, Charles M. Clark, was born October 8, 1834, at Manlius Square, New York. He graduated from Albion Academy, where he also studied medicine. He also graduated from the University of New York City Medical School in 1857. He tried to start a practice in Chicago for several years before deciding to leave on his "Trip to Pike's Peak" in the spring of 1860.

It was into the flood of almost 100,000 "Pikes Peaker's" that Dr. Charles M. Clark joined. Although he was swept with the same "gold fever" as everyone else, Clark was more realistic, more educated, and more knowledgeable than the vast majority of other men coming to the new "diggings." Fortunately he was also a very good writer. The journal that he kept is therefore considered by many to be the best contemporary account of what came to be known as "The Pikes Peak Gold Rush" of 1859-1860. He made copious observations from the time he left on his trip, therefore extensively describing the trip along the northern route to Colorado (what was called the "Denver Road") through what was then Kansas Territory, as well as the goldfields themselves. His travel took him across the Missouri River, west to Ft. Kerney in central Nebraska, then along the Platte River to the junction of its two forks, where he and his two companions then followed the South Fork of the Platte to Cherry Creek and the mountains.

Clark and his fellow gold seekers of 1860 were more informed and sophisticated than those who had gone to "get rich quick" in 1859. Most knew that gold wouldn't be just picked up off the ground. Many realized that the largest portion of gold was locked in hardrock quartz veins that meant that crushing mills and arrastras had to be used to free the precious minerals from the hard rock. Most knew that they faced long and tiring work. What the 1860 gold seekers didn't count on was that so many other hopefuls made the trip, making it almost impossible to stake a claim in the known mining districts. Many men scattered out over the Rocky Mountains to prospect in other places, but Clark and his group felt it advisable to stay in the known districts, as they knew they would probably be returning to the States within six months – too little time to try to strike it rich in unknown and unproven mining districts.

By the time that Clark left the States, he already knew that many groups had turned back before making it to the mountains; and worse, that many had turned back after inspecting the gold fields. The latter reported that the gold fields were greatly exaggerated; yet Clark persevered, partly out of the knowledge that he was better prepared, but also out of a desire to see and take part in this rush of humanity. His sense of adventure and curiosity is evident throughout his book, *A Trip to Pike's Peak & Notes Along the Way*. This book provides a chance for those of us today to experience what it was like 150 years ago at a time and place when all one's dreams of fortune "could" be fulfilled.

In editing and revising Clark's book we have endeavored to keep the "flavor" of his original tale; but because the original is in many ways hard to read today, we have upgraded his grammar and antiquated wording. We have also tried to explain the medical and Latin terms that he frequently used, but have more often simply replaced them with more modern English. We have also shortened some of his longer sentences (some run to a page in the original), and we have divided some of his longer paragraphs (some of which ran to several pages). We have incorporated his original Errata sheet and also used illustrations from other sources to help tell his story better. All of this has been done to make Clark's tale more enjoyable to today's reader. It is the editors' desire that all readers enjoy this true tale of the mighty Colorado Gold Rush as much as Clark evidently did while living and writing about the adventure.

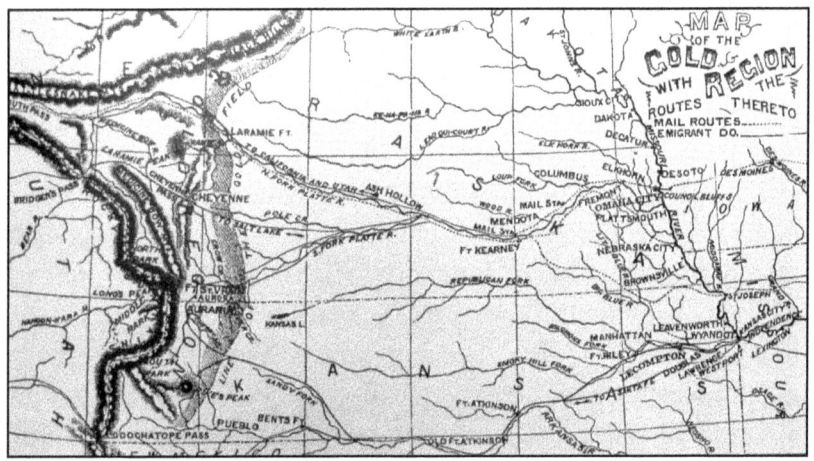

Most men used only small crude maps like this one for their perilous journey to the gold fields. Byers and Kellom, *Handbook of the Gold Fields of Nebraska and Kansas*, 1959.

LETTER I

THE CITY OF ST. JOSEPH, AND SOMETHING CONCERNING IT – VARIOUS ROUTES TO THE GOLD FIELDS – THE EMIGRANTS, THEIR OUTFITS AND APPEARANCE – APPLICATIONS FOR PASSAGE – AN ENTHUSIAST – THE FERRIES – THE STARTING OUT – A COLORED PILGRIM ARRESTED – BELLEMONT – FIRST NIGHT IN KANSAS

Many of those who started for the gold fields of Kansas and Nebraska went via St. Joseph, Missouri. Perhaps the larger number made this point their rendezvous for the purposes of outfitting, it possessing better facilities for trade and the purchase of stock than even Leavenworth, Omaha or Nebraska City. But there were a large number who found it more advantageous to proceed by way of the other river towns, and especially those who started from home with their own conveyance.

Much has been said, and much has been written, with regard to the relative merits of the several routes leading to this new Eldorado, but it is generally conceded by all, I think, that the road up the South Platte is the best and most direct. At all events, it has taken precedence over the southern, or Santa Fe (Trail), and those leading up the north side of the river.

The city of St. Joseph is finely located on a majestic bluff that rises many feet above the turbid waters of the Missouri River and from the flats presents a very pleasing as well as imposing appearance. It is regularly laid out and has many fine buildings, some of which would compare favorably in all respects, with those of larger and more opulent cities. It is reputed to have a population of 15,000, but I was credibly informed that 8,000 was a more truthful estimate. Its history dates back many years — the first building erected there being constructed by a Frenchman in 1805 for the purpose of trade with the Indians.

The emigration to "Pike's Peak" last spring (1860) differed in many respects from that of the preceding year. It was much larger in point of numbers, better equipped, and composed principally of a better and more determined class of men, who were better fitted to endure the fatigues and brave the dangers of the way, as well as better prepared to work after reaching the mountains. Many of them had started on the expedition with brave hearts and willing hands and with a determination to go through, no matter what obstacles interposed, no matter what news those who have abandoned their search for gold might bring.

There were many, however, of a different stripe; men not fitted for the undertaking. Some had come from the enclosures of a shop or an office with physical powers far below the ordinary standard, and who were unsuited for the occupation of miners and totally unprepared for the initial hardships of crossing the plains. Some, again, had started with no means for providing a comfortable outfit, having expended all their money for a passage, which would leave them destitute at the mountains. There were some even in the decadence of life—men decrepit with the burden of years, with shrinking muscles and shaking nerves, who were tottering on to the gold fields with spirits seemingly as buoyant and hopes as bright as those of their more youthful competitors. I chanced to meet several of these remnants of by-gone generations — one of whom informed me that he was eighty-three years old. His equipment for the journey consisted of a cart destitute of cover and a pair of ancient looking bullocks.

"My friend," said I, "what can induce a man of your years to undertake such a journey? Do you think you can stand it?"

"Stand it! My old timbers have tuk me thar once, and I reken they'll do it ag'in."

"What do you intend doing out there? Going into the mines?"

"Yes, I reckon ef the rheumatiz don't hinder. I made a claim thar last year up in Greg'ry's and should a made right smart ef it hadn't been that I was taken sick for more than three months; but as 'twas, I hammered out of my quartz enough to get home af'in, besides having something to roll out with this spring."

Our party subsequently overtook this old veteran near the "Cut Off." He had three passengers aboard his cart and was making slow progress, owing to his "rheumatiz" and the tender feet of his team.

There were others en route, who were literally traveling on their muscle, dragging hand-carts, rolling barrows, or packing themselves; and there were undoubtedly many who were traveling on their nerve and muscle in another sense, but it is vain for me to attempt a description of "who went and how they went," for I could not do the subject justice, and perhaps the reader has known and seen as well as myself.

After reaching St. Joseph, the bone and sinew of our party were called into action; there was the (railroad) car to unload, the wagons to set up, and their load to be regulated. Besides, there were many secondary matters to attend to; and several days passed before we were ready for the start, during which time we were visited by many curious and inquisitive brother pilgrims—the first salutation invariably being "Going to the

Peak, eh!,'' which was generally followed by a run up and down the gamut of impertinence such as – "Where you from, stranger?," "How many in your company?," "Got horses or cattle?," "Many going from your section?," "Expect to make a pile don't you?," etc.—and perhaps before leaving they would charitably remark that "That 'ere wagon's too light, it'll never stand the journey with that load on, will it, John?," (referring to some contemporary for corroboration). John, perhaps, didn't know –"timber was pretty good, but wouldn't like to warrant it." Sometimes, when just passing time, we would saunter out among the migrating fraternity—look through their camps—into their wagons—and to one keenly alive to the sense of the ridiculous, there was a treat.

There, in a kneeling attitude, surrounded by diverse articles of camp furniture and with shirt sleeves rolled up, was a brawny fellow engaged in mixing bread. Now and then a huge volume of tobacco juice came trailing out of his mouth, the spray, of course, falling short of the mark and entering the pan; now reaching for more flour, then more water, failing every time in getting the requisite quantity—but soon the proper consistency was gained and then came kneading—and such a

In their desperation to get to the gold fields, some men walked the whole distance pushing a wheelbarrow full of their meager possessions.
Frank Leslie's Illustrated Newspaper.

kneading, it reminded one of working with (making candles). It was rolled, and thumped, and fingered, and fisted; then pulled and spat upon, until it fit into the bake kettle, and the mess was over. In his near vicinity stood another specimen of the humankind, cleansing a set of greasy tin plates with cold water. The operation consisted of, first, the application of hard soap well rubbed in; then submersion in water and friction with the hand, and now and then a little scraping with the finger nails; after which they were subjected to a rub with the towel and pronounced clean.

On the sides of a wall tent nearby was inscribed an advertisement done with red chalk:

"HO for Pikes PEEK

Passingers Wanted

Board Through to Denver

For 25 DOLLARS

Inquire Inside"

NB WHISKEY for SAIL

We thought that before the whiskey "sailed" we would apply.

During our stay in St. Joseph we had several applications from men who wished to work their passage. Among them was a middle-aged man, who stated that he had just come in from the plains and had been in the employ of the government from Fort Laramie in the capacity of driver. Of course we had many questions to ask concerning the feed, the Indians, and about the gold fields, all of which were answered much to our satisfaction. He spoke of Denver City with a good deal of enthusiasm. Said he—

"Gentlemen, Denver is to be the greatest city on this continent. Why, you'd be surprised to see how it has grown within the last six months; it hasn't a parallel anywhere. Large brick blocks are being erected, and it has now some of the best hotels this side of New York City; and you'll see fine carriages rolling about the streets and some finely dressed women as you would meet with anywhere; and it is destined to be (now mark my word for it) the greatest commercial center as it is now the geographical center of this western hemisphere. Railroads are going to center there, the Platte River will be made navigable, and in less than ten years the capitol will be removed from Washington there. Mark it. You may think that I'm foolish, but I've traveled, and I know about how things will turn out." Before he had finished, the odor of bad whiskey became apparent and the nose of a bottle protruding from a side pocket, accounted for his brilliant ideas.

There are two steam ferry boats in operation on the river at this point. One runs directly across to Ellwood; the other to Bellemont, a distance of five miles up the river. The fare by either is the same, viz: six shillings, or six bits (seventy-five cents), as they term them, for a yoke of cattle and wagon, or a span of horses and wagon—no additional charge being made for the persons accompanying. Both ferries were equally well patronized; some preferring to cross at Ellwood, where the road leads up a low bottom some six miles before it traverses the bluffs; while others went by Bellemont, thus saving five miles land travel, but having a very high and precipitous bluff to climb immediately after leaving the boat.

It is quite amusing to witness the proceedings of a company who are about "starting out." All is bustle and excitement; many things are to be done which the novice little knows how to perform, but in the doing commits a dozen mistakes. There is the camp furniture to be taken care of; the stove to be cleaned out (which is generally effected by turning it upside down and getting burnt in the operation); the pots and kettles have to be packed away, and it is generally done so effectually that it will take time to find them, unless someone should happen to remember where they were put; the bedding is rolled up; and the tent is struck. Finally the cattle are brought up, when "all hands" and generally a few outsiders are called into action, and the scene that transpires is ludicrous in the extreme. Many of the cattle have been lately purchased, and nothing is known of them except the recommendation of the seller that they will work in the yoke and are perfectly kind so far as they know; but now that they are brought for trial their little individual peculiarities become provokingly manifest. Many of them are wild "harum scarum" animals, that evidence but little disposition to submit to the yoke and require a strong guard to keep them within bounds. The process of yoking commences but is conducted under difficulties, which are in part attributable to the inexperience of the operators and in part to the hard to handle subjects. Some of the old veterans yielded kindly, but the majority needed a great deal of coaxing and even then could not be brought to terms, running here and there, stepping in between those that were yoked, or taking a stampede over the commons, accompanied by vociferous shouts to "Head him off!" or "Stop him!", together with a little genteel swearing by way of emphasis. Much trouble often resulted in not knowing the right places for the cattle, and many were the labored attempts to drive the "off ox" on the "nigh side," whereby much thumping and pounding resulted.

"Get in there, you old villain! You'll come to Limerick (your leader) before I'm done with ye, I'll bet," says one. "D__n y'r eyes, you never ought to have been an ox, you should have been a jackass," says another. "Wring his tail," interposes a third, until finally the idea that "perhaps he don't belong on that side," rescues the much abused animal, who kindly submits to the yoke on the other side.

As soon as the operation is completed, they are driven to the wagons and hitched on. This is accomplished after a manner, the novice, of course, experiencing more or less trouble in bringing his team to the pole; for, if the cattle are not well broke, they will invariably go wrong. At last, all being in readiness, the word passes to "roll out," the most experienced driver taking the lead.

Our party was in readiness to take the four o'clock boat via the Bellemont Ferry. Approaching the landing, it was apparent that something unusual was transpiring. On inquiry, we learned that a Negro, en route for the "Peak," had been arrested, and not having his papers, had been taken to the calaboose. Considerable sympathy was manifested in his behalf, but no measures were taken for his rescue, and he was conducted to prison—all his golden dreams and speculation "nip'd i' the bud" by the remorseless hand of the law. I furthermore learned that the probable sequel would be his sale back to slavery, the proceeds going into the treasury for "educational purposes."

Bellemont is a small town on the frontier of Kansas, the few scattered buildings comprising it being located on the slope and ridge of a lofty bluff that rises almost perpendicularly from the river. The road leading up this "small mountain," at the time we first traveled it, had been but little worked and was exceedingly difficult to climb. We christened it "Mountain of Misery," it being the scene of an accident to our rolling stock that delayed us several hours. Since then it has been cut down to a more moderate grade, making a much better road of it. The town has grown rapidly since the advent of the Pike's Peak emigration, and speculation in city lots runs high, it being the principal business transacted there. Frequent importunities and opportunities are bestowed on the visitor to get eligible lots—corner lots—in what is destined to be the heart of the city, but which are now the silent retreats for vagrant swine and poultry in search of hazel nuts.

We were in Kansas—bloody, bleeding Kansas—the late scene of political strife and civil war—the "harp of a thousand strings," each strung to a sorrowful pitch, and which every political demagogue knows how to finger; and which has shed throughout the length and breadth of the land, not the "soul of music," but the sound of discord. The whole territory presents a vast, uneven surface of prairie, poorly watered and sparsely timbered, over which high winds continually sweep—where hurricanes flourish and frolic, and fierce storms rage. The soil, however, is good, possessing all the elements of a rich soil; and agriculture might flourish if the climate were suitable, but it is now subject to frequent droughts that devastate the country, and in some portions of the territory, the possibility of living is entirely precluded. That portion bordering on the Missouri River is generally exempt from the many evils that brood over the remainder; the bottom lands being very productive. The timber is all confined to the borders of the streams and consists principally of cottonwood, some oak, elm and black walnut.

We prepared to spend the night on the ridge of the *Belle-mount* and located our camp opposite an institution that was designated as a "Bakery, Grocery and Provision Store," which supplied us with eggs, milk and bread for a reasonable compensation. This was the initial step of our camp life, and where we were first initiated into its mysteries as well as miseries. Our sheet iron stove was set up, the cooking utensils and dishes brought forth, and the cuisine department was established; then one person scoured the commons for fuel, while the other proceeded half a mile down hill for water; after which the coffee was set boiling, the potatoes baking, the meat and eggs frying, and while one superintended these operations, another set the table, laying the covers on a small portion of a city lot. At last the repast was pronounced ready, but night had fully asserted supremacy, and a tallow dip was brought forward to illuminate the several matters for discussion before the squatters—and we were all squatters for once from necessity—the dignity of a chair would have been ridiculous.

To tell you how food relishes under these circumstances would set anyone with bad digestion crazy, a glance at the vacant dishes would convey an idea. After supper, the pipe, that symbol of peace, was produced to mitigate the fullness of a burdened stomach and to solace our nerves after the fatigue and excitement of the day; and as the smoke rolled in wreaths around and above us, it carried on its bosom the gilded fabric of a truant mind, whose proportion grew with each succeeding puff. But alas! The foundation thereof was smoke, and our towering castle fell; and, tired of life's mysteries and miseries, we looked amid the ruins for a comfortable place to sleep, but there was not much choice in the pallet Dame Nature had spread nor did we deliberate long on "foreside" or "backside" but wrapping a blanket 'round us, and looking aloft to see if there was any prospect of rain before morning, we lay down with the song of the whip-poor-will for a lullaby to dream of home and feather beds.

LETTER II

GENERAL CHARACTER OF THE ROADS—WHO LIVES IN KANSAS, AND HOW THEY LIVE—THE DROUTH OF LAST SEASON—TROY AND THE TROJANS—TOO MUCH LOAD ON—HAVE TO RAZEE THE WAGON BOX—STAMPEDE F STOCK—WOLF RIVER—THE GRASSHOPPER—KICKAPOO INDIANS—THE BIG NEMAHA—VISITED BY AN OLD GOSSIP—HOW SUNDAY PASSES IN CAMP.

The roads through Kansas are a vast series of ups and down, and in looking out over the vast unbroken surface of the prairie, one is reminded of the huge swells of the ocean, and the wagons (justly termed schooners) perform about the same motions in traversing it that a ship does in riding over the waves of the high sea—now toiling up one, then dipping down to ascend another, in tedious succession. Now and then, an unbridged slough presents its mud and mire, but which has to be crossed, and in the endeavor it proves a "slough of despondency" to many, being often the scene of trouble as well as accidents. One, I distinctly remember, proved disastrous to us—so much so that we were obliged to keep it company for thirty-six hours.

The road itself is, from the nature of the soil, hard and smooth in dry weather, the soil being a mixture of clay and sand; but a little rain changes it materially, it becoming soft and slippery and difficult to travel. For some distance back from the Missouri River, the country is well settled and bears the impression of enterprise and industry. The farms are general under good cultivation, well stocked and enclosed by good fences; the buildings are well constructed and look neat and comfortable; but, as we precede farther back, the scene changes, and one begins to realize that he has passed the boundaries of civilization and has entered the realm of the Indian and the buffalo. Occasionally, to make the desolation more apparent, some squatter's shanty rears its lonely shelter, surrounded by a few tilled acres, and looking as lonely as a hen coop at sea and about as insignificant.

Many of the "settlers" in Kansas emigrated there during a political furor following in the wake of Jim Lane (a Kansas abolitionist), and many have been lately introduced there through misrepresentations of the country; and they now would give their land, improvements, and all to get back to the States again—and many are going back. In conversation with one who was returning, I learned that he had been in the territory nearly two years; had been located near Centralia; had tried to cultivate a farm, but could not raise crops; said he had been induced to go there through false representation; had been told that there was plenty of water and a good climate—all of which was a d__d lie in every particular, and he was going back to Iowa.

The drought of last season impoverished the whole country; nothing grew or matured, except on the bottom lands, and that was principally corn. A prominent citizen of Seneca, a lawyer, informed us that the crops in their immediate section of country had failed, and the same was true elsewhere so far as he knew. He also stated that the heat during the summer months had been excessive, the thermometer often marking 119 degrees in the shade.

Letter II

"Why, gentlemen," said he, "to live and to move required no mean exertion; the air came to our nostrils as from a seven times heated furnace; the water in the streams evaporated, and all vegetation was burnt up. We have had no vegetables to eat this summer and not much of anything else; and it might stagger belief if I were to tell you that there were men here, educated men from the classic halls of Yale and Harvard, who have been and are now living on dried buffalo meat and crackers. Now I don't pretend to live here, nor do I intend to stay long; I came here about a year since, like many other young men who could not get a living in the States and commenced pettifogging (handling petty cases), but it doesn't pay. If I do business for a man, he tells me that he has no money, but that he has got a cow or a calf that he will give me or something else. There is no society here; the majority of the people are illiterate. One-half the men that I do business for, when called upon to sign an instrument, have to make their mark being unable to write. We are cut off from all communication with the world, except once a week, when the mail arrives, bringing the *New York Tribune,* which is *the* paper."

"Do all the residents here feel as you do?" we asked.

"The majority do, and all who can close up their business and get away are going to look for another boarding house."

"What do you think are the prospects for this country?"

"Not very brilliant for the present, but in time I have no doubt but what it will improve and will be settled up. But I have noticed one thing—all the good and desirable men now go and will continue to go north of the fortieth parallel of latitude. The country is better and the climate is better; the country south of this parallel is less desirable and is populated by a scurvy set of Missourians and Hoosiers, who are as ignorant of what is decent in nature as a hog."

Troy is a small town, located some nine miles west of Bellemont, comprising a blacksmith shop, several whiskey shops, so-called groceries, etc. It is a pretty location, on the summit of a hill, is the county seat, and is surrounded by a well-settled country. The Trojans receive their principal trade and support from the emigrants, as well as the other towns along the line of travel. On reaching this point it became evident that we were carrying too much load; the axles had sprung, and the surmise was that our running gear would be sadly crippled unless we took immediate measures to lighten up. But how, was the query. We had no stock that we wished to dispose of, having already left a quantity in store at St. Joseph that we could not carry, and we could not sell to advantage. So it was decided to keep our stores and cut down our wagon box, it having a broad upper projection and a false bottom, which could be dispensed with; and to work we went. The wagon sheet was removed, the hoops taken off, and the load unshipped.

While we were thus engaged, we were joined by a party consisting of Mr. R____, his daughter and aged mother. They wished to travel in company with us, as they had lately been insulted by a set of drunken loafers whom they had just passed. We expressed our perfect willingness, if they could await our readiness, and as our arrangements would not be complete before night, they encamped and were directed to wait until morning and take an early start. The morning brought a cold drizzly rain with all the attendant discomforts; our breakfast was delayed; our clothing got wet; the high wind that prevailed came near stripping our wagon sheet; and, to cap the climax, as we were about ready to start our horses took a stampede. We had just taken breakfast in hand, when our attention was called to our little dog, which was playing with the lariat of one of the horses, but before we could interrupt his sport, the horses had taken fright and were off at full speed over the hills and across the stream, where they were lost to view. We lost no time in

Letter II

following but after losing sight of the horses, we ran at random, and for a time the chances of regaining them looked dubious. Some of the party, fatigued with the chase, gave up in despair; but finally the horses were found at a distance of three miles having been caught and secured by a farmer. We brought them back, immediately hitched up and started out, our confidence in horseflesh much shaken.

Three hours' drive brought us to Wolf River—a stream of some magnitude in the spring, but during the summer it shrinks to a mere brook. Its borders are densely timbered, the approach to it is steep and rugged, and the bottom is stony; much care in driving therefore being necessary for a safe fording. After leaving this stream, we crossed several narrow ones tributary to it and also passed several small towns. At length we reach the Grasshopper, an important stream at certain seasons. The approach to it, on either side, is high and precipitous; its western border furnishes the best camping ground to be had on the whole route—plenty of wood, good cold spring water, and a splendid grove of timber composed principally of slippery elms, the barks of which look like a hotel register with the carving of names. The country surrounding is known as the Kickapoo Reserve, a small tribe of Indians living here, numbering some three hundred. They are partially civilized and have the teachings of a missionary. They are small in stature and dress after the manner of civilians, but there are only a few that can talk intelligibly.

After leaving the Grasshopper, we pass one or two small streams, which afford good camping places and going a distance of seven and half miles reach the small village of Capioma, the abode of a set of vampires who suck subsistence from the poor emigrant. A Mr. _____, when returning from the gold fields, was taken sick and obliged to stop at this point. He was taken to the Gage House, where he remained four days; at the expiration of which time he was able to proceed. His bill was presented, amounting to thirty dollars, being charged five dollars per day for board, with the item of ten dollars for professional services rendered by the doctor, and withal the storekeeper had a small bill for sundries, etc. Being destitute of money, the sale of his wagon and horses was insisted on, for which the storekeeper offered sixty dollars; and, there being no alternative, they were thus sacrificed, leaving him a balance of twenty-five dollars to get home with. This account was furnished me by a farmer living in the vicinity, who was well acquainted with the transaction, and he stated that the whole establishment was well worth a hundred dollars more than was paid. This is not the only instance of "falling among thieves" that has occurred on the road, for the whole route swarms with "sharpers", demons and devils, who are ever ready to take advantage of the necessities of any man.

Proceeding on from Capioma, we reach, at a distance of four miles, the junction of the Leavenworth road. At this point is located a house of entertainment designated as the Pacific House. At a distance of a mile and a half farther on, at the foot of the second hill, is located what is termed a "ranche." When we passed through, water was scarce—slough water at that—and they were retailing it here at five cents per glass, with whiskey enough thrown in to disguise its bad taste and smell and to cut its slimy consistency. Six miles farther travel over heavy hills brings us to a large stream, the "Big Nemaha," which is bridged. Above the stream, on the western side, lies the respectable town of Seneca.

We reach this point on Saturday and encamped to spend the Sabbath. The borders of the Nemaha afford good camping ground, plenty of good spring water, etc. Before night set in we were joined by several companies, among which was the Chicago Leader Company, or better known as the Rounds

Letter II

Company. We had made their acquaintance at St. Joseph and now hailed their appearance with emotions of gladness.

Sunday came in bright and glorious, bringing the reprieve so anxiously awaited from the fatigues of a wearisome journey; but there was nothing, save in our own consciousness, to mark it as the Sabbath—no church bell awoke the stillness of the morning with its call to worship, for there was no church, and the inhabitants of the far west don't consider that they want such institutions; they have not thought of Sunday as yet, and the majority of the emigrants think of it only as a day to rest their stock and change their shirt, and some forget even this.

A Sunday in camp on the plains passes with a careless abandonment. Various are the ways in which it is spent. A peep into the tents will discover the manners of some, while a look through camp and the vicinity discloses the manner of others. In the tents we notice a variety of occupations; some are engaged with needle and thread, in patching up the wear and tear of their trousers; others cleaning their revolvers, covering their meerschaums (pipes), and sharpening knives. Here is one laid away on a pile of blankets, recuperating the wasted energies of the past week in sleep; another is mending his boots; and another, for the want of something better to do, is complacently viewing his sun-burnt face and the growth of his beard before a small edition of a large glass. Outside some are having a glorious game of euchre (a card game) seated around an inverted water-pail; some are engaged at target practice with rifles and revolvers; others are washing their dirty clothes; and a few may be seen seated on the wagon tongues or leaning up against the wheels, their long, sad faces indicating a severe attack of nostalgia. They are thinking of the comforts and blandishments of home and undoubtedly wish themselves back again. The scales are beginning to fall from their eyes, and instead of looking through the false medium that the imagination had furnished when seated around the home-lit fire, they are beholding and experiencing the stern reality. The pictures their fancy painted in bright and glowing colors are fading and assuming a slightly greenish hue; the road is not paved with golden sands, but common dirt; the sky is not always serene—heavy and foreboding clouds sometimes darken it; the air is not always bland—fierce and howling winds often sweep over them. In fact, the courage that nerved their hearts around the comfortable fire-side, when contemplating the journey, is leaking out; and "I want to go home!" is legibly impressed on every feature. Poor humanity! You should have looked long and well before taking the leap.

On our return, and while encamped on this stream, we were visited by an elderly woman who came into our camp with curiosity sparkling in her eyes. Says she—"Going to stop in these parts?"

"Not long," we answered.

"O, you've come from the Peak, eh? Well, how's matters there, ennyway?"

We satisfied her on these points, and thinking it our turn, we asked, "And who have we the honor of addressing?"

"Oh, I'm Widow _____, everybody knows me – just live over there."

"Well, how long have you lived there? If we may ask?"

"Well, now, I'll tell you," and she prepared to give us a general outline of her history. "I came here 'bout four years ago, determined to get some land, and I've got it. Why, I've entered, and been the means of entering five quarter sections, besides an eighty, and I done it pretty sharp, too; and all I had, don't you think, when I got here was six hundred dollars. When I

Letter II

first came here, there was nothing here, and I went to the river and bought a load of provisions, and don't you think, it cost me two hundred dollars. Well, then I put me up a house and planted twenty acres of corn and hoed it and done it all myself, and here I be sixty years old and hain't known what it is to be married for twenty years; and, don't you think, after my corn got to growing, and was e'en a'most big enough to cut, the (Mexican-American) War come, an' the soldiers took it all for their horses, and many more things that I had, and it cut me pretty short, but I got a start agin."

"How has the drought affected you?" we ventured to ask.

"I hain't raised a thing this year, but I've managed to get along; and I'm going to take some of my stock to the river and sell it, and I just come out to look up some of it. You hain't seen nothing of a red steer pass this way, have ye?"

We informed her that we had, and that it went into timber, and she started in pursuit of the "pesky critter" at a full lope. This woman was an Amazon of strength and energy and had accomplished more than half the sterner sex could boast who were located around her. She was possessor of a thousand acres, some of which was valuable, it being located in town, and she was going to cling to it, wouldn't sell a foot of it—and furthermore, as she stated, "She did not run for the war, and she was not going to for the drought" but was going to remain, confident of better "times" next year.

LETTER III

ASH POINT—WHICH IS THE BEST ROAD TO FORT KEARNEY—VERMILLION CREEK—SOMETHING OF A STORM—AMONG THIEVES—SOME IDEA OF THE EMIGRANTS, AND THEIR TROUBLES AND TRIALS—THE WOMEN AND CHILDREN EN ROUTE—ACCIDENTS, POVERTY AND DISTRESS—THE BIG BLUE RIVER AND MARYSVILLE—STAMPEDERS—VICIOUS HABITS PRACTICED BY PILGRIMS.

On leaving Seneca, the road leads over some very high hills, and we pass several small streams before reaching Ash Point, a distance of eight and a half miles. At this point the road forks, the right hand road leading through Oketo and designated as "The Great Military and Freight Road to Fort Kearney—the shortest and best route, saving twenty miles in distance." The other is "The Great Military and Stage Road to Fort Kearney" and leads through Marysville and is the most traveled. Considerable strife has existed here between the partisans of the rival roads. Just before reaching here a man had been shot for expressing his opinion as to which was the best road. The cause of the strife is said to be purely political.

As to which is the best road, I am not able to say, nor can the traveler have confidence in the statements of those who are interested. The road leading through Marysville is the one traveled by the stages and by all of Major & Russel's freight

Letter III

Lots of men walked to Pike's Peak pushing or pulling hand carts with their possessions and the tools that would be needed to do their prospecting.
Frank Leslie's Illustrated Newspaper.

trains, and from my knowledge of it, I can pronounce it a good road, the country it leads over supplying plenty of water, wood and good forage. At a distance of nine and a half miles from Ash Point we cross the line into Nebraska, and four miles farther travel brings us to Vermillion Creek, where there is a stage station. We encamped here for the night, in company with many others, among which was a train returning from New Mexico, and one en route for Denver City. Soon after camping, a violent storm of wind and rain broke in fury upon us, which came near carrying away our tent and lasted some two hours. After the storm had abated, the wagon-master from one of the trains came to our camp and informed us that thieves were abroad and cautioned us to keep an eye on our horses, or we might lose them. The night was intensely dark, and just such a night as would favor the stampeding of horses and mules. We needed no second warning but proceeded for our horses and brought them into camp, securing them fast to the trees; we each then took turns in watching with instructions to shoot anything human or inhuman that was seen lurking on the borders of the camp; but the night passed without disturbance, and the early morning found us again on the tramp over the vast open prairie. During the day's drive, we passed and saw a great number of emigrants.

The emigration to the gold fields of Kansas and Nebraska (now Colorado) last year was large; by actual count at Fort Kearney for several successive days, an average of two hundred wagons passed daily, with an average of four persons to the wagon, and this was kept up through the months of May and June. One can imagine how the road was traveled, and what a thoroughfare it must have been. The road had an average width of thirty feet of well-beaten track and was as smooth and hard as a brick yard pavement, excepting some portions along the Platte Valley. It is undoubtedly the best natural road in the world, some portions of it where it traverses the ridges being as level as a house floor; and often did we imagine that a *Flora Temple* in harness would just please us; at least it would have been a great relief to have got behind something that could cancel distance a little better than an ox team and end the tedious journey.

It was on these ridges that the wind wagon made its best time. This vehicle consisted of the ordinary running gear, only made very light; at each end were two upright poles, or masts, each of which carried a sail, which supplied the motive power. Four men occupied this machine, and they informed us that they had traveled as many as one hundred and sixty miles a day. Of course they had to drag it over the hills and through the sand, which was decidedly hard work. I have often seen a continuous train of wagons reaching for miles ahead of us, their wagon sheets in the reflected light, looking like sails; and we could almost fancy them a fleet of vessels, especially when seen amid the glimmer of the rising heat, which often deluded us into the belief that we were approaching a stream of water. This ascent of rarified air is peculiarly exhibited on the plains, rising to an altitude of three and four feet from the surface of the prairie, in wavy lines, and seen in the enchantments of distance, its resemblance to water is almost perfect.

The troubles and trials that are encountered in passing over the plains are numerous, but not more so than one would naturally look for and expect, considering the state of the country, but they are not of so grave a nature as many imagine them. Most people in the States have an idea that an expedition to the Rocky Mountains is attended by great peril and consider that it is tempting Providence to undertake it. The most serious trouble, as well as the most frequent, was the stampeding and loss of stock. It was no unusual thing to encounter men who engaged in looking up lost horses, mules or cattle, and often did we

"hearken to the hurried questions of despair,"

as to whether we had seen any of the missing articles, but it was seldom indeed that we could give them any information. If the animals had strayed, there was a possibility of finding them; if they had been stolen, their recovery was past hope.

The loss of a man's team on the plains was a calamity not only feared but dreaded. They were, in one sense, his only salvation; without them he was left to the tender mercies of his fellow travelers, and I am sorry to say there was not much sympathy manifested towards the unfortunate; every man was too much engaged in attending to his own interests to help others. Imagine the feelings of a man who has suffered this loss; he has accomplished half of his journey, when, through some instrumentality, his cattle or horses have stampeded; he starts in pursuit, little knowing where to look, and the day passes in agonizing and fruitless search. His eye roams over the broad and barren plain but no traces of the lost, he starts into the bluffs, follows up the canons, traverses the devious windings of their many chambers, now and then ascending their summits to look abroad over the plain, but the fleet antelope and the sneaking wolf are the only objects that meet the eye. He starts back to his encampment with the dark shades of night and despair settling thick around him to meet the anxious family, some of whom have also been engaged in the search, but with a like failure. He has but little money; those with whom he had been traveling could not wait and have gone; and as he reflects on his almost hopeless condition, hot, scalding tears fall and course down his cheeks. Another day follows a sleepless night, and he starts out again to take a wider circuit with a renewed hope; he questions the travelers as they pass, but they have seen no stray animals, and the intelligence falls like a nightmare upon his heart. He takes another course, hoping against hope; climbs the bluffs again and again, suffering for water and ready to drop from fatigue. At length his search is rewarded; back upon the high prairie are the objects of his solicitude, calmly feeding, and with glad cries of "Eureka," which awakens the slumbering echoes of the hills, he hastens them back to renew his journey. But all were not thus fortunate in finding their stock and were obliged to buy a team from some of the emigrants or get freighted through.

Accidents to rolling stock were frequent, causing delay and trouble. Axles would break, and tires would require cutting and setting. When an axle broke, it was exceedingly difficult at times to find timber sufficiently large from which to make a new one. I have known as high as ten dollars to be paid for a stick for that purpose. Ox-yokes were frequently fractured, and bow-pins often slipped from their place; and the ox, glad to be free from his burden, would run and caper, requiring the united efforts of the company to secure him. Crossing the sand was a trial that tested the patience of the emigrant, it being

Letter III

often necessary to "double up" in order to effect the transit, and then it was troublesome, occasioning more or less fretting, swearing and pounding of the poor jaded brutes.

It was often interesting to look about you and see who your traveling companions were. The emigration was, to some extent, cosmopolitan in its constitution. You would frequently encounter the apathetic German, with the everlasting pipe in his mouth, the witty but careless Irishman, the lively Frenchman, the sedate Englishman, now and then a Swede and Norwegian, together with the ebony-hued son of Africa, and last, though not least, the speculative and wide-awake Yankee, who is determined to go through or bust in the operation. Old and wrinkled age was there and rosy youth, and, withal, the mewling infant in its mother's arms. The women and children were well represented, for many a man was so confident of success that he was moving his family, and it is remarkable with what fortitude they endured the discomforts and trials that attended the journey. Many of the women were clothed in bloomers, but the majority exhibited the good old-fashioned long skirts but without hoops and other fashionable deformities. I have seen them in the early morning tripping gaily over the prairie in high glee or riding on horseback; and some even had shouldered the ox-gad and were driving several yoke of cattle with all the professional glib and ability of an "old hand."

The little children were objects for pity, harmless and helpless as they were, confined to the limits of the wagon night and day; sometimes parched by heat, sometimes shivering with cold, and often suffering for the want of water. Verily, I looked upon a man as *non compos mentis* (incompetent), who was subjecting his family to the discomforts and hardships of so long a journey over an almost unknown region of country; and I still maintain that any man who removes his family from a comfortable home, packed like so many "dry goods" behind an ox-team, across the plains, and with nothing but an "expectancy" for their maintenance after reaching the mountains, is eminently entitled to be considered as suffering from aberration of mind.

The emigrants traveling across the plains were not exempt from personal harm; "accidents would happen" there as elsewhere and many of them were of a most serious nature—especially those resulting from the careless use of firearms. Every man, when starting out on this expedition, considered that a rifle, revolver and knife were as essential as flour and bacon; and they were provided accordingly—the two latter secured by a belt to his person, while the other idly swung in the wagon, all loaded and ready for use. This practice of wearing a small armament girded about the person was general, and it appeared most ridiculous. It looked as though every man distrusted his neighbor, and this was pretty generally the case; and, as the

Some of the more unlucky men didn't make it to Pike's Peak. Indian attacks were rare, but they did happen, and the bodies were just buried by other travelers along the road.
Harper's Weekly.

result of a quarrel, instead of resorting to a fistic encounter, the revolver was appealed to, and in the hands of the passionate, the results were often sad.

The rude slab at the head of many a grave bears the inscription, "Accidentally shot," either by his own or a friend's carelessness in the use of fire-arms. There were many that received injuries during the stampede of mules and horses, getting severe contusions and in some cases fractured bones; but I have never heard of any loss of life from this cause. Beyond Fort Kearney a few miles, a little child while leaning out of the carriage window, lost its balance and was precipitated head-foremost to the ground, receiving injuries from which it soon died, although receiving every attention that science could bestow while under the care of Surgeon Summers at the fort.

Poverty was exhibited in all its rags and filth on the plains, and it was distressing to notice the many that were suffering from the want of clothing and sufficiency to eat. Many had started upon the expedition with a few pounds of flour and a little bacon—not sufficient to take them through—and had to rely on their wits and the charity of their fellow-travelers. Many had no suitable clothing for their feet, their sad remnant of shoes being braced up and held together by strips of cotton cloth. Their blankets had been pawned for bread, and some even had parted with their only coat to obtain something to appease hunger. I was told of one instance where a man would go to the feed boxes behind the wagons and gather the scattered kernels of corn that had been left by the animals and eat them to keep from starving.

The encampments of emigrants were often visited by persons who would report that they had started out in the morning ahead of their team, and that it had not yet overtaken them, or that by some means the team had got ahead of them, asking for supper and lodging, which was generally granted together with breakfast in the morning; but it was found that these persons were generally imposters, having no connection with any team or company, resorting to this method to get through.

On leaving Vermillion Creek, the road leads over several high ridges, and at a distance of seventeen miles we reach the Big Blue River and the town of Marysville. This is the largest town on this line of travel between St. Joseph and Denver and is growing rapidly, having increased one-half in population and in number of buildings since we passed through last May. It is located on the eastern side of the river, the buildings being scattered in patches across the valley from the river bank to the bluffs. The buildings are all frame, with the single exception of a large two-story stone dwelling situated at the north-eastern extremity of the town.

The Big Blue River is also the largest stream that we meet with that we cross. Its banks, in some places, are densely timbered with Cottonwood, several varieties of Oak *(Quercus)*, together with Black Walnut *(Juglans Niger)*, Ash, Willow, etc. The approach to the stream is quite steep and in fording the river you follow down the channel several rods before ascending the opposite bank. During high water it cannot be forded, but there is a rope ferry provided some little distance up the river that is put in operation during a freshet. The river at the place of fording has a width of fifty feet or more, and at low water does not exceed two feet in depth.

Before reaching this point, we had met several parties returning back to the States; they were called "Stampeders" and were made the targets for the "outward bound" to shoot at, and many were the shafts sent at them; the finger of scorn was often pointed at them, and many a derisive laugh grated harshly again their tympanums (inner ear). Some had been through to Denver, and considering that matters looked rather squally, beat a hasty retreat, thus frightening others, who turned before accomplishing half the distance. One party of young men, I remember, turned about before they had proceeded thirty miles from the Missouri River, not having sufficient courage to cope with the hardships that presented.

The Stampeders were generally ashamed to meet those who were pursuing their way to the mountains and would shrink back under cover until passed; but they were generally hailed and inquiries instituted. Some would jocosely remark that the "Peak" had broken off; others that they were returning for provisions but were going to eat them at home. Some pronounced the gold excitement a hum-bug and stated that the quartz mills were good for nothing but "old iron." Later on we met these persons by scores daily; in fact, there was nearly as many on their return as there was going. The inscriptions on their wagon sheets were various; some, who on starting had written "Pike's Peak or Bust," now added the *"ed,"* absolutely *busted*; others had inscribed "Bound for America," etc.

The emigrant, in traveling across the plains, acquires many debasing habits. I do not wish to be understood as saying that all do, but then all are more or less lax in their morals. Many who had never before indulged in the use of profane language or in draughts of whisky soon learned to intersperse his conversation with big oaths and to smack his lips after a swig at "Old Bourbon" with a decided relish. Smoking and chewing tobacco, together with drinking a quart or so of strong coffee at a meal, were other accomplishments—they were the necessaries.

Sunday was by many entirely disregarded; the majority had seemingly left all their humanity and their morals at home, bringing along their brutality and all the evil propensities of human nature, and those most moral at home were generally the most abandoned abroad. They were under no restraints, far away from the benign influences of home and civilization, surrounded by all conditions of men and manners, and as man is an imitative being, it is not strange that he was insensibly coerced into practices that would have shamed him in the community he had left behind. They apparently lost all pride of character, as well as pride in personal appearance, not caring how they looked or acted; and it was generally remarked, "If you wish to develop a man's true character, bring him out on the plains." There was no masquerading there; crossing the plains was the furnace that tried him, the scales that weighed him, and if he was found wanting, it was soon known—no man's reputation could cover up his true character. If he was prone to be irritable, cross and peevish, it was soon evinced; if vicious, the propensity was sooner or later manifested.

A party of men do their nightly choirs along the trail and relax (often with a little whiskey) after a hard day's work.
The Illustrated Miner's Handbook and Guide to Pike's Peak.

LETTER IV

HOW WE TRAVEL AND HOW FAR A DAY—HOW CAMP IS MADE—COTTONWOOD CREEK—SEVENTEEN MILE POINT—THE GAME, SEEN AND HUNTED—SICKNESS, AND SOMETHING ABOUT THE DOCTORS—LONE PRAIRIE GRAVES—ROCK CREEK—AURORA BOREALIS—ROAD-METRE—TABLE OF DISTANCES.

Traveling over the plains, when going out with a load, is necessarily a slow and tedious process. No matter whether you drive horses, mules or cattle, there is not any material difference—for you cannot go faster than a walk and do justice to your team. The majority of the travelers left camp at about seven o'clock in the morning and would travel until meridian, unless the day was sultry, when they would turn out at eleven and rest until two o'clock; then they would proceed on until six o'clock, when they would encamp for the night, provided wood and water were at hand. During our journey out, we endeavored to get as early a start as possible, but the hour for leaving camp depended much on circumstances. The first duty of the morning was to "loose" the cattle and turn them out to graze; the next was to provide breakfast; when this was dispatched, the tent was struck, the bedding folded up, the camp furniture gathered, and all was packed away in the wagon; then the cattle were driven into camp and yoked, and we started and would travel eight or ten miles before stopping to let the cattle graze and provide lunch for ourselves; or provided that there was a more desirable camp and better forage ahead, we would continue on until that point was reached, then unyoke the cattle and turn them out to feed. The mess box was then brought out, and the contents noticed, each disposing of himself as his feelings dictated. After lunch some amused themselves with a game of euchre, others at chess, while the balance "turned in" under the wagon for a nap. After an hour or two had elapsed, or as soon as the cattle were pronounced full, we made our arrangements for starting again and would continue on, sometimes riding but more frequently walking until six and sometimes seven o'clock, when we turned out to encamp, having traveled a distance of eighteen or twenty miles. This was the average travel; however, we sometimes have traveled twenty-five or thirty miles a day.

At about the hour for encamping, the master of the train started ahead on the pony to look for a suitable place and when found would return and pilot the train; and on reaching this spot each wagon was drawn up so as to form a "corralle," or enclosure. This method is adopted by all large trains, for the reason that it facilitates the yoking of the cattle, for when driven within it they are more easily controlled. This arrangement of the wagons also ensured greater safety in case a storm arose during the night, for each braced the other, and they could be chained together, which is often done. The smaller companies, with their four to six wagons, did not often attempt the formation of a corralle, and when they did, it was a signal failure for it requires much practice in driving cattle in order to bring the wagon into position. The majority did not know how and seemingly could not be learned.

After the wagons had been drawn up in order and the cattle turned loose, the tent was unfurled and "pitched" and the stove set up. If there was no wood in the vicinity, as was often the case, several would start and search for the *"bois du vache"* (literally, "drink of a cow"), or "chips," as they were termed and bring them by armful into camp; these made good fuel and furnished a hot fire, but in the burning, the abundant residue of ashes so clogged the stove as to require a frequent cleaning out; and then the odor they sometimes exhaled would have put anybody but a pilgrim out of concert with his appetite for supper.

After the meal was prepared and eaten and before darkness set in, the cattle were generally driven up, unless they were thought secure, and roped and then tied to the wagon wheels. Then, sometimes, a camp-fire was lighted, and the members of the company would squat around it, to talk over the incidents of the day or else engage in spinning yarns until bed-time, when all but the watchman took up his bed and started for the tent to bunk down on the hard, unyielding surface of "mother earth;" but first the revolvers and knives were looked to and strung on the ridge pole, in order that we might be ready in case of emergency.

The camp at night presents a strange appearance; and strange scenes are often enacted owing many times to the disordered fancies of the watchman, who frequently sees more with the optics of the mind than the natural eye—a clump of bushes often assuming the proportions of a man who is sneaking into camp, or a bunch of waving grass is transformed into the likeness of a wolf; and many a time has the camp been thrown into utter confusion by the ringing report of a pistol shot, which had been fired at some suspicious object, awakening the various members of the company, who start up and run out with very many tangled ideas of "What's up?," rushing in to fill up their opening senses. The watchman, as a matter of course, has an exciting story to tell of a man he'd seen slyly creeping over the bluff or along the river bank with "most foul intent," or a wolf had entered camp and he had shot at him but just missed him;

how one ox had jumped over another in a fright, etc. After learning the full particulars, the majority returned to bed, but a few remain to chaw or smoke, in order to calm their perturbed minds.

After leaving the Big Blue River, the road leads over a country similar to that I have described in the preceding letters. The country is very well settled, especially along the borders of the river, and I judge it to be very productive; but this section of country seems to be especially subject to violent storms and tornadoes. No less than two or three swept through there the past season, destroying everything they came in contact with, un-roofing houses and scattering their timbers far and wide, prostrating fences, killing stock and doing immense damage.

At a distance of twelve miles we reach Cottonwood Creek, a small stream which is dry during the summer months. The approach to it is winding and steep, and as the bed of the stream contains several large stones at the ford, some care is necessary in driving. There are two good springs here but no wood. The stage company has a station here, and there are also one or two other buildings. On leaving this stream, a series of long but gradually sloping hills have to be crossed for a distance of five miles, when we arrive at a good camping ground, known as Seventeen Mile Point, where there is a well of water besides a good spring and plenty of wood.

The game seen on the plains is not as plentiful as one would naturally expect; but very little is seen along the line of travel; now and then a small herd of antelope are seen grazing near the bluffs or passing down to the river, but so shy it is almost impossible to get within rifle range of them without resorting to a decoy. Anything red in color will attract their attention and draw them, and a person wearing a red shirt can hunt them more successfully than another, if he will take a position and

Letter IV

remain quiet. They were incessantly hunted, for their meat is considered a great delicacy, being very sweet and tender. During the months of May and June many young kids were found and brought alive to camp, and some endeavored to raise them, but they generally failed. They make pretty pets, and many are seen at the ranches on the Platte Valley, domesticated. Elk were occasionally seen, also the jack rabbit, which is fully as sly and agile as the antelope. Buffalo were seldom seen during the spring and summer months, but in the month of September they are seen in large numbers. I shall speak of them more fully in another letter. The bird game was more plentiful, consisting of grouse, quail, snipe, plover, sage hens, etc. Ducks were sometimes plentiful on the river.

There was many a nimrod among the traveling community, and numbers might be seen daily passing over the bluffs to gratify their passion for hunting; and it many times led them into difficulties—some getting bewildered, turned around, and lost. I have known several instances where men have been obliged to spend a dismal night amid the bluffs, their company miles away from them; and some have never returned, being murdered by the Indians. Starting out alone into the bluffs after the tantalizing antelope and wolf was perilous business without chart or compass; one was often bewildered, not knowing where to go, and was subject to being robbed and often murdered by bands of roving Indians, and when overtaken by night there was no alternative but to lay down, hungry, thirsty, suffering from fatigue and fear, to await the morning sun—their only companions howling wolverines and swooping night hawks.

Sickness often visited the emigrant. The prevailing diseases were bilious fever, which often assumed a typhoid character, pleurisy, pneumonia, and scurvy, besides many other incidental ailments which were excited into action by exposures, insufficient and improper food, and over-exertion. Many were suffering from rheumatism, opthalmia, etc. I mentioned scurvy as one of the prevailing diseases but do not remember having seen a pure case; it was often, however, a complication, and I neglected to state that diarrhea and dysentery were prevalent.

Owing to the very indifferent accommodations offered to the sick, who were carried along day by day in the wagon, bolstered up on the top of the load, exposed to all the vicissitudes of weather and travel, their diseases that under more favorable circumstances would have excited no alarm and would have yielded kindly to treatment became alarmingly aggravated, and the physician, when called, found it exceedingly difficult to speak of the result even in cases that under ordinary circumstances were invariably curable. Not a few succumbed to their disease, dying away from home and friends in the wilderness. That distressing distemper of the mind, nostalgia, which was invariably lit up on the approach of any bodily malaise, exercised a most baneful influence, seemingly paralyzing all life and hope, filling the mind with corroding fears and prostrating every vital energy; hence suspending all recuperative efforts and in many instances counteracting and preventing the effects of every medicinal agent.

The services of a doctor could not at all times be obtained, although there were many of the profession en route, but they were continually on the move like the rest, and it was difficult to tell where to find them. Every man, however, had a package of drugs and nostrums (quack medicines) with written directions for use, sometimes consisting of blue pills, a little ipecac and opium, together with a bottle of peppermint, pain killer, and somebody's "sovereign remedy for all ills." But they often hesitated in their use, and perhaps it is well that they did, for I cannot but consider that medicines in the hands of

Letter IV

those who are totally ignorant of their nature and of the indications that call for their use is productive of much harm. They are sufficiently hazardous when administered *"secundum artem"* (according to your skill/ability) at the hands of the accomplished physician, and I would advise all who contemplate taking this trip to leave the item of drugs behind; if they take anything, let it be some domestic prescriptions that they are well acquainted with. They had better trust to their *"vis medicatrix naturae"* (force is nature's healer) and a cheerful disposition, than all the elements of the *"material medica"* (medical material substance – more generally, the body of knowledge about a drug of therapy). There is no reason why persons should suffer sickness in crossing the plains, if they are at all observant of the laws that govern their system, any more than at home, and none need be if they would pay more attention to the quality and quantity of food used and be more careful in the matter of exposure.

The medical profession was well represented, as I have before mentioned, but I do not know that their number exceeded the limbs and branches of the law, who like their medical brothers had tired and grown thread-bare in waiting for practice and were passing out to a less contested field with a hope to recuperate their finances. Some were connected with quartz mills and were going into the mines—had thrown "physic to the dogs," having served an unappreciative public long enough. Others, with an eye to practice, had their names inscribed in big letters on their establishment—the ominous M. D. having a two-fold significance, not only implying that he was a *"Doctoris Medicena"* (Doctor of Medicine), but that "Money Down" was required. In some instances the mortar and pestle were exhibited over the name, signifying *"In hoc signo, vince"* (or, Conquer under this sign – the message given to Constantine by God in a dream).

Seldom had a day passed that we did not see one or more graves beside the road. They were often visited by the traveler—flinging a shadow o'er his heart and reminding him that Death held his court there as well as in the crowded city. These graves, owing to the hardness of the earth in some localities, could not be sunk very deep, and many were buried in a trench scarcely two feet in depth without coffin or shroud, being rolled in their blanket and laid away to their final rest. I was told of one instance where the grave was so poorly constructed that the occupant's feet had been seen protruding out. Many were undoubtedly poorly buried, but generally the best disposition that a Christian spirit could dictate was made of the last remains of a fellow traveler, being decently buried, and a headboard erected bearing the occupant's name and where from, either inscribed by a pencil or carved with a knife. Every one visiting a grave would make a note of their visit on the board, and sometimes would inscribe an epitaph; many boards were literally covered with them and with the names of visitors.

Near the Pawnee Ranche are three graves side by side, situated upon a little rise of ground, each enclosed by a railing, and at the head of the middle one is a marble slab, the only one seen on the whole route. On the Platte Valley are three other graves, where repose the last relics of D. Thompson, Q. Stanley, and D.W. Brown, from Iowa; all three were killed by lightning while sitting in his wagon, killing him instantly, and setting fire to the wagon; the horses were prostrated by the shock but received no other harm. What a sad termination of life! To be cut down in the midst of hope and health by a scorching thunderbolt, and no man could say his end might not be like his. All were alike exposed, and the occurrence of a thunder storm excited fears in the strongest hearts, for who could say that ere another morn they might not be—

Letter IV

"Perchance a thing,

O'er which the raven flaps his funeral wing."

The next point we make is Rock Creek, where there is a stage station and several dwellings. It is thirteen miles distant from Seventeen Mile Point. The creek is spanned by a good bridge – ten cents being charged for crossing — but it is optional with the traveler whether he cross by the bridge or ford the stream, the banks of which are very steep. Either side of the creek affords good campground, and there is plenty of good spring water and wood to be had. It was here, on our return, that we witnessed an exhibition of the *Aurora Borealis*, which far surpassed anything of the kind I ever saw. Heavy clouds had been sailing past all day, but as night came on they had settled down, belting the horizon with a somber zone, while above peered forth the bright and smiling faces of heaven's constellated host. We reached the station at midnight, but previously our attention had been directed to a brilliant light in the north, which was considered as reflection of a prairie fire, but as it momentarily increased, and we could see the fingers of light reaching higher and higher, that supposition gave way, and the true nature of the phenomena became apparent. Soon the whole heavens became ablaze as it were, the electrical points irradiating from the north and west and piercing the very zenith, now retreating, then starting up again with the brilliancy of outline that was dazzling, their whole length presenting shades and colorings from the pale straw tint at the base to a brilliant scarlet at the apex, magnificent to look upon; and the moon, just rising from the heavy drapery of clouds, lent new beauty to a scene which was richly worth the whole journey to witness.

In traveling across the plains, one's attention is frequently directed to the heavens. You seem to be under a new firmament—the planets and stars shine brighter and appear

The men, women, and children who went to Pike's Peak all had their dreams of "striking it rich," but most were going because they were dirt poor and needed the money to survive.
Harper's Weekly.

nearer, owing doubtless, to the purity of the medium through which they are seen.

After leaving Rock Creek, twenty-two miles travel over a desolate country brings us to the Little Sandy. There are several ranches and sloughs intervening.

In giving the distances to these various points, I am governed in party by my own judgment and the judgment of others. There is, perhaps, not matter wherein men so much disagree as in the matter of road distance. You ask a man how far 'tis to such a place, he will tell you so and so. Another, if asked, will say that is not so far, or farther. You do not know which to credit but split the difference and travel. Much depends on the manner in which the road has been traveled—if with an ox team, he invariably adds a mile or two more than the man with the horse team, judging of the distance by the time taken to cancel it. The table of distances inserted here are nearly correct, and as near as they can be ascertained without resorting to actual measurement:

TABLE OF DISTANCES
St. Joseph to ....Miles
Bellemont 5
Troy 8   13
Small Creek 1   14
Wolf River 6   20
Bear Creek 10   30
Claytonville 6   36
Grasshopper 9   45
Capioma 6   51
Pacific House 4   55
Seneca, (or Big Nemaha) 8   63
Ash Point 12   75
Vermillion Creek 13   88
Marysville, (on Big Blue) 17   105
Cottonwood Creek 12   117
Seventeen Mile Point 5   122
Rock Creek 13   135
Little Sandy 22   157
Big Sandy 4   161
Little Blue 52   213
Elm Creek 16   229
Clark's Ranche 8   237
Platte River 18   255
Fort Kearney 10   265
Shakespeare 19   284
Plum Creek 15   299
Willow Island 15   314
Smith's Ranche 8   322
Stage Station 4   326
Gilman's Ranche 3   339
Cottonwood Springs 15   354
Jack Morrow's 12   366
Bishop's or Fremont's Station 12   378
Fremont's Springs 8   386
Bob Williams, (O. Fallon's Bluff) 6   392
U.S. Mail Station 2   394
Pike's Peak Stations 16   410
Lower Crossing 20   430
Upper Crossing 22   452
Lillian Springs 27   479
Beaver Creek 50   529
Fremont's Orchard 41   570
Fremont's Hill 3   573
Saint Vrain's Fort 41   614
Denver City 44   658
Golden City 65   723
Gregory's 24   747

LETTER V

LITTLE SANDY AND BIG SANDY – SOMETHING ABOUT SNAKES, POLECATS AND VERMIN – THE LITTLE BLUE – WILD PLUMS – BAITING FOR WOLFES – PAWNEE INDIANS – FLIES AND MESQUITOES – THE PLATTE RIVER AND VALLEY, AND SOMETHING CONCERNING ITS NIGHT WATCHES

The Little Sandy is a small muddy stream, very serpentine in its course, having steep approaches and bounded on each side by very heavy hills. Located on its western bank is what is termed "The Little Sandy Hotel," built of hewn timber; in connection with it is a small grocery, where whisky and tobacco may be obtained, these being the most staple articles and not likely to "spoil" by long keeping. Corn may also be obtained here, when there is any in the country. A few miles further travel over steep hills, we reach the Big Sandy. The approach to it is very gradual and easy. There are several buildings erected here for the entertainment of the traveler, and there is also the relic of an old log bridge spanning the stream. This stream is quite broad but shallow, its depth of water not exceeding two feet except at certain seasons. At the time we forded, it was considerably swollen, the water reaching up to the wagon box. The flat on its western side affords a good camping place, there being plenty of wood and generally good feed. The water of the stream runs with a stiff current and is generally clear, but its banks swarm with sand flies and mosquitoes.

Letter V

The plains, as one would naturally suppose, has its compliment of loathsome reptiles but not to the extent that I had imagined. Their ranks have been thin for the past two years and are daily getting thinner, for the whip and cane of the emigrant has been at work dealing death and destruction to the hated snake. We see but few rattle snakes, and those are principally the small prairie kind; but occasionally we meet with the large, active, yellow species, which are more formidable. The (water) moccasin is sometimes met with, but the most common snake is what is termed the bull snake; these are a large, sluggish snake, averaging from three to seven feet in length, having a large head and a bright spotted skin; they are said to be harmless. There are also many other varieties, among which may be mentioned the black snake, the adder, the common striped snake, grass snake, etc. Cattle are sometimes bitten on the road by the rattle snake, and when they are, they are left to die; but it is very seldom that they are so bitten, for every snake seen is suddenly dispatched by the driver or some one of the company, and every one esteems it fun to be in at the death. They are sometimes found within the camp, and when so found; every suspicious looking hole is stopped up for some distance around, for the idea of visits from such neighbors during the night is anything but agreeable. When a rattle snake is killed, the rattles are taken off by the superstitious, who believe them to be an infallible preventive of the headache if worn on the person.

Pole-cats are numerous, especially on the borders of the Little Blue River. It was here, on our return, that we were annoyed by them. They seem to have a special fondness for wild plums, for while encamped on the borders of this stream, we gathered a large quantity of these plums, and the animals would visit us every night, bringing a perfume that all the spices of Arabia could not sweeten. One night I was awakened by the fierce and continued barking of the dog, and looking out of the tent to ascertain the cause, I spied a skunk under the wagon deliberately engaged with our plums, now and then reaching up and poking several out of the open bag, then settling back to eat them, manifesting no uneasiness at the barking of the dog, whom he occasionally eyed with all the nonchalance of one who didn't scare easily. Thinking that I could easily frighten him, and cause him to abdicate, I hallooed and threatened but to no use; his looks and actions said plainer than words could have expressed it, "There is no terror in your threats!" His perfect *sang froid* (cold blood) completely upset me, and the query was how to dislodge him. I dared not resort to harsh methods, for I already began to smell consequences, and thinking that discretion was the better part of valor in this particular instance, I left him to his feast, thinking that he would soon overindulge and go. But the morning still found him there, his capacity seemingly undiminished, but on seeing several of us issue from the tents, he slowly walked away. As soon as he reached the limits of the camp, he was shot, and we hastened from the infected locality, not having an appetite for breakfast.

In traversing the plains, one wonders at the various manifestations of life that are everywhere present—every square foot of surface has its visible inhabitants. Countless ants are traversing the country in pursuit of winter supplies, and their travels are frequently extended to your own person; we see them in all sizes and various colors—red, white and black, and some are winged. Many of them throw up large conical hills, consisting of gravel, and it is exceedingly interesting to stand over one of these mounds and watch them rolling out huge particles of gravel and fixing it in place. Myriads of grasshoppers jump and flit around you, and often do we get a stroke in the face from some specimen who is taking a flying leap. Spiders, fleas, bugs and every variety of insects are numerous. In some localities I have seen clouds of spindles sporting in the air. Innumerable butterflies are also seen during the summer months of every hue and color and as gay and brilliant as the flowers they flutter

Letter V

amid. The flies and mosquitoes of the plains at certain seasons constitute the greatest annoyance that the traveler is subjected to. Of the former, there are many species besides the common house fly, there are horse flies and ox flies, and the green and blue-bottle fly. Of horse flies, there are two varieties—one is large and of a grayish speckled cast and inflicts a most cruel bite, sometimes attacking men; the other variety is quite small and fastens itself around the eyes and nose of the animals. There are several varieties of fly that attack cattle—one is very large, measuring fully an inch in length, black in color, and a most expert vein cutter; they are not numerous, and it is well that they are not, for they could soon destroy an ox. The green fly is the most numerous class and more indiscriminate in its choice of food. I have seen dead carcasses by the way completely covered with these flies, and our camp would often swarm with them, and while partaking of our meals they were most disgustingly familiar.

The mosquitoes and gnats are still more troublesome, as their attacks are made during the night, but we were by no means exempt from them during the day; so numerous were they in some localities that it was found necessary to tie the cattle up and build smudges around them. Every camp that we made on the Platte Valley on our return was infested, and smudges and smoke did not mitigate the nuisance for their continued and discordant piping was more dreaded than their bite. Their numbers seemed infinite—no sooner was one division dispatched, than another succeeded.

> *"Though hundreds, thousands bleed,*
>
> *Still hundreds, thousands more succeed."*

We would often give up in despair and propose to leave camp, the poor brute animals faring less well than ourselves. I have seen cattle completely covered with them and so irritated by the bites that they could not feed but would commence to travel, sometimes running and rearing with pain; horses and mules were continually rolling to rid themselves of the tormentors. Often have we found it impossible to remain at certain places through the night and would hitch up and drive until morning and then lie by and recruit ourselves and teams.

The return of night was dreaded—to us it brought no healthful slumber or rosy dreams, but *au contraire* (on the other hand), it was fraught with teeming horrors, for no sooner had the first bars of night fallen, than the dancing commenced, and we had to face the music—and such music. Heckling entertainments were soothing in comparison. Our efforts to keep them without the tent were in vain, and we would almost narcotize our system in trying to stifle them with tobacco smoke. The only manner in which we could get a wink of sleep was to cover our heads, and this was decidedly unpleasant, when the thermometer was indicating 96 degrees. The gnats and the small flies by day were often very annoying, small bodies of them continually floating before you, diving at your eyes and nose, and it was not infrequent to swallow some, if the mouth were open.

The Little Blue River, or the American Fork as it is sometimes called, is a very pretty stream, having a deep but narrow channel, and, withal, very serpentine in its course. Its banks are skirted with several varieties of timber, among which may be mentioned the Cottonwood (*Populus Augustifolia*), the long-leafed Willow, blue-foliaged Ash, and the quaking Asp (*Populus Tremulaides*). Along some portions are to be found dense thickets of small Plum trees, which yield a fruit little inferior to that of cultivated trees—the pulp of the fruit, when fully ripe, being very sweet and of delicious flavor. The cuticle or skin, however, differs widely from that of the tame plum, it being thicker, denser, and possessing the peculiar astringent characteristic of all wild fruits. Grapes are also found in abundance, the vines trailing and interlacing among the branches of the trees, forming many pleasant arbors and retreats that are very inviting to the traveler. The distance from the Big Sandy to this river is fifty-two miles; the intervening road is rolling for a portion of the way, but the balance crosses long level ridges, perfectly flat, where the eye wanders vainly in search of tree or shrub, but over which was scattered a profusion of flowers—their rich and variegated colors contrasting grandly with the broad, emerald surface of the ridge. Here it was that we first noticed specimens of Cactus (*Opuntia Vulgaris*), or Prickly Pear as they are termed.

On our return trip, we delayed at this stream several days for the purposes of sporting and recreation. Vast herds of elk used to roam over the bluffs bordering on this stream, but now there is seldom one seen. Wolves, however, are plenty, and also the small coyote, and during our sojourn on the Little Blue we turned our attention to baiting for them. There are three kinds of wolves that roam over the broad plains of the West—the gray wolf, the coyote (or common prairie wolf) and the buffalo wolf. These latter are very large, black in color, having long shaggy hair, and follow after large herds of buffalo. The coyotes are the most numerous and live on the open prairie. Gray wolves are also numerous; these and the coyotes band together. I have frequently seen numbers of them in the early morning, fighting and snarling around the carcass of a dead bullock. They are often seen at night around the camp of the emigrant, and they sometimes attack horses that are lassoed out; several instances of this kind occurred last year. When traveling at night, it is no unusual thing to be followed by a pack, whose howling make the night hideous, but they seldom or never attack men. We were once so followed while crossing the sand hills, but they kept at a respectable distance and did us no harm.

Baiting for these animals is being made a business of by the proprietors of ranches, who are located on the Platte Valley, during the winter months. The manner of baiting is to obtain a fresh carcass of antelope or deer, cut it open, and then trail it along the prairie for some distance, now and then cutting off a portion of the meat and throwing it down after having dosed it with strychnine. After dragging the carcass sufficiently far, it too is thoroughly poisoned and left. As many as fifty wolves have been thus killed during the night.

On leaving the Little Blue, the road follows up the northern bank of the river over high rolling ground for a considerable distance, and we pass several ranches, among which may be mentioned Harrington's and Ropen's. The latter is denominated the "Pawnee Ranche and Store." It is through this country that the Pawnee Indians roam. Many of them during the season for buffalo hunting encamp on the banks of the river. We saw several of their provisional encampments; the lodges

. The broad Platte River was followed for much of the way, and the Indians that were seen were usually begging for food.
Harper's Weekly.

Letter V

are constructed of a frame-work of bent poles, each extremity being sharpened and set in the ground—the hole covered with boughs and twigs, which are secured by bands of willow bark. They are arranged in circles, and I have counted as many as seventy-five arranged in a group on a small plateau of ground back from the river. The appearance of the camp is pleasing, being arranged with all an Indian's taste for locality, and the many huts with their coverings of thick green foliage; resembling as many arbors which you might fancy as the homes of the wood-nymphs, if it were not for the dusky forms of the warriors seen in and around them.

The Pawnees were the first Indians known to the whites in this region of country, being visited by Dutisne (a French explorer) in 1719. They were once a large tribe, but in 1832 the ravages of the small pox diminished their number by one-half, and their ranks are being thinned every year by the murderous assaults of the Sioux and Cheyenne. They are a warlike tribe, courageous and brave and 'tis said that one Pawnee warrior will whip six Sioux or Cheyenne. Their sole dependence is hunting, stealing and begging from the emigrants.

On leaving the Little Blue River, a few hours travel brings us to a stage station, sometimes called Clark's Ranche; but we have passed in the meantime a small creek known as Elim or Elm Creek, at which point there is a remarkable depression in the prairie, once the course of a stream of some importance, the high perpendicular banks of which are cut up and divided in many grotesque forms, and which wind in various directions. At Clark's Ranche there is noticed similar basins. At this ranche there is a good well of water, and it is important that the emigrant should here fill his cask and water his stock, for he finds no more that is fit to drink until we reach the Platte River. The road from here passes over a high ridge for a distance of twelve miles, when we reach the sand hills that border on the valley of the Platte or Nebraska River. After passing through these, a distance of a mile or so, we catch our first view of the broad valley of the Platte River. As we pass on, we may be said to enter the second division of our journey, for we are about to traverse an entirely different country. Six miles more travel across the valley brings us to the bank of the river, where we encamp for the night.

The Platte River is a very broad but shallow stream—its name, La Platte, designates its great width. It is sometimes called the Nebraska; this is an Indian word and has the same signification, meaning "flat" and was used by the Indians to designate the broad and shallow river. Numerous islands are found in this stream, some of which are very large and clothed with an abundance of grass. The timber skirting the borders of this river is in some places very heavy, but above Fort Kearney there is not much to be found, except it be on the islands or on the northern border, and the emigrant has to depend solely on the absinthe or the *bois du vache* (cow patty) for fuel. Its channel is in some places quite deep but is continually shifting and changing, thereby rendering navigation, even in small canoes or boats, quite uncertain and troublesome. In some places the channel is completely lost, the water disappearing under the quick-sand, and owing to its quick-sand bottom it is unsafe to allow cattle to remain standing in it long, as they settle very fast. This river presents a magnificent appearance, and one is likely to imagine that it might be made navigable, but this is an eternal impossibility; however, it is said that the steamboat El Paso in the spring of 1853 ascended it some five hundred miles; if this feat was accomplished, it was not done without much trouble, which must necessarily have occurred, owing to the nature of the stream. It has a fall of some six feet to the mile.

Letter V

The valley of this river is very level and has a width varying from three to ten miles, being bounded on either side by high sandy bluffs, which are very picturesque in appearance, some of them terminating in innumerable peaks. The supposition is that this valley was once covered with water, and the appearance of many of the bluffs evinces that such was once the case, for the old water marks are still visible, where the water had surged and washed and then receded, repeating the process until the waters finally subsided to their proper channel, the sides of the bluffs being cut up into a series of steps resembling a staircase. The many shells and stones found on and around these hills, afford other evidence that they were at one time covered with water. I have often found pebbles and stones of various colors and kinds that have been worn perfectly smooth by the friction of the water, and many of them, from their peculiar composition, could only have come from the mountains, having been thrown there by a mighty rush of that element at some time. The valley is at times closed in by ridges of sand, which are hills of difficulty to the emigrant, it requiring a long pull and a strong pull to cross them.

One of the essential conditions for safety in crossing the plains is the establishment of night watches. Every company, after leaving St. Joseph establish as a rule that each member shall take his turn in guarding the camp at night and no postponement on account of weather, considering that "eternal vigilance" is the price, not only of their own safety but that of their stock. The company with whom we traveled instituted a night and morning watch, the one commencing at the hour for retiring (which was very irregular) and lasting until 1 a.m., when the other came on, lasting until sunrise. On the approach of night, the question circulates as to "whose watch tonight?," but as no memorandum is kept of the matter, it is hard to say. If one should happen to have a presentiment that it is his, he keeps mum, hoping that the duty may devolve on his neighbor, for, as might be supposed, the watching o'-nights is not very agreeable after the fatigues of a day's travel. The matter get a little mixed, but it is straightened, and before bed-time, for the majority of the travelers have very retentive memories as regards "whose turn it is," and, after a little argument, and many words, the matter is adjusted. If there happens to be any member who is suspected of napping during his watch, he, in turn, is watched and if caught when slumber is sitting heavy on his senses, he is securely bound in his position, and a great outcry is made, pistols are fired, etc., which awakens the vigilant subject in affright. A scene of course ensues, which is richly enjoyed by the company, who have withdrawn to witness the outcome.

LETTER VI

FORT KEARNEY—LETTERS FROM HOME—
KEARNEY CITY—HOW EMIGRANTS ARE
TREATED—BUFFALO AND BUFFALO HUNTING—
SMITH'S RANCHE AND THE RANCHES ON THE
ROAD—HOW THE INQUISITIVE ARE ANSWERED—
SIOUX INDIANS, THEIR ENCAMPMENTS, ETC.—
STAGES AND STAGE STATIONS—PONY EXPRESS—
GILMAN'S RANCHE, AND WHAT OCCURRED THERE.

Fort Kearney is considered by the emigrant as the great intermediate point between the Missouri River and Denver City. It is the place he looks forward to after "starting out," for there he expects to get news from home. This fort is located at the head of Grand Island and about two miles back from the river. It was removed here at the suggestion of Col. Fremont, and this locality was chosen in preference to any other, because this island and the river is well timbered; aside from this, the situation has no advantages. The fort's buildings are located on the open plain and about midway between the bluffs and river; the buildings are principally frame with now and then a mud or sod house.

On reaching this point, the emigrant feels that he has reached an oasis; he sees once more the evidences of civilization and refinement, the neat and comfortable tenements of the officers, the offices and stores, all remind him of home, and as he looks aloft to the masthead, where the stars and stripes are proudly waving to the breeze, he fully realizes that he is still protected and still inhabits America. There is a post office and a hospital established, in part for the benefit of the emigrants. The former is located in a small mud building, and for the benefit of future emigrants, I will state that the postmaster is not as courteous and obliging as he might be; but perhaps the dignity of his position and the rules of office do not permit him to be gentlemanly to what he considers the poor, plebian gold hunters. On making inquiry for letters, ten to one, if you are not eyed with a suspicious look and then referred to the list of "advertised" pasted on the walls. If you expect papers, it is needless to ask for them, for he is the proprietor of a news depot and considers them as his property; and should you happen to reach the office near his dinner hour, you are told that he cannot wait on you, but that he will be back in half an hour or so.

As the emigrant is not allowed to encamp within two miles of the garrison, he either proceeds down to the river or passes on to Kearney City, a distance of two miles from the Fort, and twelve from the point where we first strike the Platte River. This town is composed of a few mud houses that are occupied as groceries, etc., and there is also a blacksmith's shop. These mud houses, as they are termed, are constructed of blocks of sod, and this is the principal building material in this region of the country. These blocks are laid up tier after tier, to form the walls, which have a thickness of two feet; when these walls have been carried up sufficiently far, a ridge pole is erected, and then a series of small poles are laid across to support a layer of sod, which constitutes the roof. These houses are comfortable, being cool in the summer and warm in winter, besides being very durable, lasting twenty years or more—their cost is from three to four hundred dollars. The outside surface, in order to preserve it from the weather, is coated over with a preparation of lime.

Letter VI

The plain on either side of the town affords pleasant camping ground, and plenty of good well water can be obtained. Wood is scarce, as government will allow no timber to be cut, and the residents have to obtain their supplies some fifteen or twenty miles distant.

It may be interesting to many to know how the emigrant is treated while pursuing his lonely way over this forlorn country that is, for the most part, inhabited by as scurvy a set of bipeds as ever demoralized any community, and I refer now principally to many who have squatted along the line of travel for the purpose of genteel robbery. Some little idea may already have been gathered from the small circumstance that occurred at Capioma, which I referred to in a previous letter.

The emigrant has generally many little wants to gratify while traversing the troublesome way, and he expects to pay for them; but when he is called upon to pay five and twenty percent more than residents, it is an imposition. This was often demanded throughout the settled portions of Kansas, where one might naturally hope for better treatment. The majority of emigrants were considered as a low thieving set, too poor to be honest; and, in fact, many of them were poor in the commodity that buys respect, and they were treated accordingly. While at Kearney City, a man entered the blacksmith shop for some article; after he had gone, the proprietor turned to his employee and said—"I want you to watch these d—d pilgrims, they'll steal—keep your eye on 'em!" This was a charitable assumption toward a customer and a stranger too, but this remark evinces the general feeling toward the class that travels the plains. It is thought a good joke to insult and quarrel with an emigrant, and they will not scruple to take the advantage of a man with knife or pistol.

After leaving Kearney City, we have a good level road to travel, which leads up the valley about midway between the river and the bluffs, but which at a distance of six miles leads to the river border, where we have an opportunity to water the stock. The river at this point is fully a mile in width and contains quite a number of islands. Thirteen miles farther travel brings us to a ranche, called Shakespeare's, but it has no accommodations for the traveler, except if he wants a mixture of whisky and river water; but few, however, want the compound, for the majority carry a plentiful supply of "corn juice" and seldom take it any other way than raw.

While turning into camp at this place, we saw a wolf coming down to the river to drink, and several of the party started out to have a shot but had not proceeded far before the wolf turned and started for the bluffs at a full gallop; one of the party then mounted a pony and gave chase and succeeded in heading him off at the base of the first range, some three miles distant, and gave him two shots from his revolver. Neither took effect, and the wolf made good his escape, much to the disappointment of all the party, who had been greatly excited in the chase, intensely hoping that the wolf might be killed and brought into camp. All our efforts at wolf-killing during forty-two days of travel across the plains were unsuccessful. I have many times started out in pursuit of these animals, following them over the bluffs and through the defiles, but never succeeded in getting anything more than a good sweat and a mile or two behind the train.

During the day we saw several buffalo and also noticed quite a number of the skulls of this animal scattered over the valley, bleached perfectly white by the long exposure, many of them being penciled over with the names of those who had preceded us. But few buffalo were to be seen during our passage out; but in September, when we were returning, we saw vast herds of

Letter VI

them, and I presume that I have seen fifty thousand of them scattered over the high prairie back of the bluffs. Vast herds were also to be seen in the valley, apparently as tame and fearless as so many cattle; they would often block up the road and stand regardless of our approach; and often have we set the dog on them and scattered more or less lead among them with our revolvers, but which had no other effect than to cause them to rear up and *stampede.*

Hunting the buffalo, or bison, is sport and was so considered by the returning emigrant, who was to be seen daily pursuing them, either on foot or on horse-back, and it was also considered a great feat; every company that we met with were anxious to know if we had killed a buffalo. The wholesale murder of these noble creatures, for the mere sake of a pastime, was cruel, and many would kill them for the credit of the thing, having no other design; and it was not unusual to pass large numbers of these animals lying dead on the plain, wholly untouched except by carnivorous flies.

The Bison (*Bos Americanus*) possesses a powerful frame, being built very compact and strong, having two more ribs on a side

Bison were one of the sources of food for the emigrants on the plains, as they had been for Native Americans for years. Clark saw only a few of the animals on the way west, but many more on the return trip. *Harper's Weekly.*

than the ordinary ox. Its height at the fore-quarters exceeds six feet, and it will weigh from twelve to fifteen hundred pounds. Its neck, withers and chest are covered profusely with an abundance of long, black hair, which completely hides all the outlines of form and gives him a most ferocious aspect; this long hair is so arranged about the forelegs as to give the appearance of small pants. The eyes are small and brilliant, and the horns small and black. They are generally very slow in their movements but when frightened, they can run like "quarter horses" and will leap over barriers and up precipitous banks with astounding agility. I have frequently heard that when wounded, they would turn upon the assailant with great impetuosity, but this statement, made by many writers, can be qualified; they do not always turn and attack, as many, besides me, who have encountered them, can testify.

One sultry afternoon, in company with a member of our party, I started from our encampment on the borders of the river and proceeded towards the bluffs, having seen a herd of buffalo lazily grazing beneath their shadows. On reaching their vicinity, we hid ourselves behind a clump of tall grass that afforded a good screen and awaited the movements of the herd, which consisted of twenty large bulls. They soon commenced a slow march toward the river, being led by an old veteran, in single file, now and then giving vent to a horrid *bruit,* which was like the mutterings of distant thunder. As they neared our place of concealment they began to sniff and paw the earth and finally halted, but soon resumed their slow march, now and then shaking their huge heads and looking toward our locality.

We patiently waited until they were opposite, when my companion arose and gave the nearest bull the contents of his rifle, telling me to reserve my charge until we saw what effect his shot had; but he was too much excited to take deliberate aim, and the only effect his shot had was to frighten them into

Letter VI

a smart gallop back to the bluffs. No sooner had they turned than I discharged the right hand barrel of my gun, saluting the same bull with ten buck shot on the hip, producing rather a peculiar sensation, I thought, by the way he cut the air with a series of kicks; but he did not stop, following on after the herd, and we after them at full run. On reaching the bluffs, some sixty rods distant, they halted, looked around, and then proceeded at a slow walk up one cannon, while we in the endeavor to head them off took up another. Fortunately, the two channels united at no great distance, and we reached the junction first, and the leader was not to exceed five yards distant. We discharged our pieces at his head, which had the effect to stagger him, and he settled back, protruding his tongue, while his small eyes flashed and burned with passion; he was evidently preparing for an attack and assumed the position. It was a moment of intense excitement, and we were undetermined as to what course to pursue. We had but one charge left, and my companion suggested the propriety of reserving that until he could reload, unless the buffalo made the charge. But the animal had reconsidered the propriety of his course, and, as all of his companions had left him, he too turned and started off, not so badly injured as we supposed. We let him go, fearing that if we provoked him further, that our lives would be put in peril; and I have no doubt, had we troubled him further, that he would have attacked us, and as it was, he occasionally turned around, seemingly undecided where to make at us or not.

A bullet will seldom penetrate their skull, because of the thick covering of hair and hide and the density of the bone. They are also very tenacious of life—in one instance we put sixteen bullets into one before he fell, and then he rose again and staggered off a rod or more before expiring. Their meat, to my taste, is not good, being very course, dry and tough, and the only way we could relish it was to cut it into strips and smoke it, and then use it as we would dried beef. The whole Platte Valley is cut and furrowed with their many trails or foot paths, leading from the bluffs to the river, worn sometimes to the depth of three and four inches; and at some places, back on the high prairie, circular paths are seen, worn quite deep, where the bulls have stood guard at certain seasons to protect the cows and calves from the wolves.

After leaving Shakespeare's, the next point made is Plum Creek, distant fifteen miles. There was but little water in this creek at the time we passed, but the approach to it is very steep and the banks high. Passing on, we reach Smith's Ranche at a distance of twenty-three miles, but in the meantime, pass Willow Island, which is fifteen miles beyond Plum Creek. This island is of considerable size and thickly covered with low willows and some cottonwood.

Smith's Ranche is a small building constructed of logs, where liquor, preserved fruits, etc., are to be had. Why these buildings, or stations, are called "ranches" is more than I can say. The proprietors do not cultivate the soil, nor do they raise stock; they have merely squatted along this line of travel for purposes best known to them. These miscalled ranches throughout the Platte Valley are essentially one and the same thing; sometimes differing in size and in style of construction—some are of the adobe species, while others are constructed of rough logs and poles, and sometimes we meet with one built of square cedar posts, that looks very neat. The proprietors are generally rude specimens of humanity in every sense of the word, and many of them dress in garments made from elk and deer skins ornamented with long fringes of the same materials up and down the seams; their hair and beard, in many cases, have been suffered to grow, giving them a ferocious look; and in fact, they are as primitive as the country they inhabit. In order to insure the respect and confidence of the Indians, many of them have squaw wives, who inhabit a lodge erected nearby. The emigrant

Letter VI

generally makes it a point to stop at these stations and has more or less questions to ask, often inquiring about the distance to such and such a point; and it would seem that the proprietor considers the frequent importunities of the inquisitive a great annoyance, for many times we see a bulletin pasted outside, of which I present a verbatim copy of two:

"Just Looka Here"

"Don't ask any questions, for God's sake, for here they are all answered."
"How far is it to Cottonwood Springs?"
"2-1/2 miles, and 42 miles to O'Fallon's Bluffs."
"How far are we from Kearney?"
"Just 88 miles."
"How far to Denver?"
"It is 300 miles by old road, 260 by the Cut-off.?|"
"Any good water in?"
"Not a d____d drop. Good spring 80 rods beyond, on the road on the right hand side."
"Any wood at Cottonwood Springs?"
"No Sir, not a d___d bit."
"Are you a married man?"
"No sir E."
"Don't you want a wife?"
"Well, wouldn't object."
"How long have you lived here?"
"2 years."
"Do you like it?"
"Well, I does."
"What's the name of this place?"
"Fox's Springs."
"How old are you?"
"None of your d____d business."
"Have you any pies?"
"Yes sir."
"How do you sell whisky?"
"15 cents a drink. All of which is submitted.
                                          W. P. Fox

The other is rather milder—and reads:

"How Are You?"
"How far to the next ranche?"
"2-1/2 miles."
"How far to Cottonwood? About eight miles?"
"Yes sir."
"Keeping old Bach's Hall, are you?"
"Yes sir."
"Why don't you get a woman?"
"Can't find one."
"Where do you get all this cedar?"
"Up in the bluffs."
"Are we likely to come to any Indians soon?"
"No. Don't think you'll come to any Indians."
"Any fish in the river?"
"Yes, a plenty."
"What kind of game do you find here?"
"Wolves and jackass rabbits. There is more 10 or 12 miles in the bluffs."
"What part of the States are you from?"
"Vermont."
"Been here some time, ain't you?"
"Yes, think I have."
"How far are we from Kearney?"
"79 miles."
"How far is it to O'Fallon's Bluffs?"
"50 miles."
"Is there any post office on the road?"
"Yes, there is one at O'Fallon's Bluffs."
"How far to Denver City?"
"307 miles. Walk in. All questions answered free of charge."

Just beyond Smith's Ranche, at the time we passed through, was an encampment of Sioux Indians, sometimes called the Dahcotahs (sic). They are a very large tribe, one of the largest that roam over the wide waste of prairie. They are divided

Letter VI

into bands, and each band is again divided into villages, each having its chief. They are continually roving, moving their lodges every few days. These we saw here had just come from the opposite side of the river, and the squaws were very busy in unpacking and erecting their lodges, while the Indians came flocking around us with the invariable salutation of "How! How!" and asking for "baccy" (*tobacco*) and "sucre" *(sugar)*. They are inveterate beggars and seldom go away satisfied; they often want matches, and their pantomimic manner of asking for them is truly amusing, imitating the manner of setting it on fire and the method of using them. This tribe had a large herd of ponies and numbered some forty lodges, but they had not yet all arrived, and we saw a long string of them fording the river, the squaws leading the pack horses and having their arms full of brush for fuel. Their lodges are constructed of buffalo skins stretched over a series of poles, put up so as to form the figure of a truncated cone; some of them are very large, having a circumference at the base of thirty feet and more, the covering being fastened together with wooden skewers, leaving two flaps at the apex that can be closed or thrown back to allow the smoke from the fire to pass out. There is also an oval aperture left for the door, the whole being pinned down to the earth, and a little embankment thrown up to keep out the wind. The lodges are generally erected in a circle, and over the doors of the warriors and chiefs may sometimes be seen the scalps and trophies of war, while nearby is erected on a tripod of poles, the whitened shields and quivers and the medicine bag, and here and there may be seen strips of red cloth offered up to the Great Spirit as a sacrifice.

We encamped for the night about a mile beyond the ranche and had scarcely pitched our tents before we noticed several large and half naked Indians on the full run for our camp, their long black hair streaming out behind, and their blankets gathered up at the waist, leaving the upper portion of their body naked, their faces bedaubed with paints of various colors, making them look frightful. On reaching our camp, one of their numbers produced a paper covered with Masonic emblems, which was an appeal in their behalf asking travelers to bestow charity. Many are furnished with these papers, especially those representing themselves as chiefs. On coming into camp they inquire for the *"Capitaine,"* shake hands all around, and then wait silently for *sucre,* coffee, and some want flour.

We gave them some sugar and tobacco, and after we had finished our meal, gave them the remnants, together with a cup of coffee. They are great gourmands, and to see them eat, one wonders at the capacity of their stomachs; they eat all you give them but don't seem to fancy bologna sausage much.

As we pass on from Smith's Ranche, at four miles we reach a stage station. These stations are located about twenty miles apart along the line. They are constructed principally of frame work, both the dwelling and barn. There are several lines of stages to Denver City, one starting from Leavenworth, another from St. Joseph, and there is one line running through to California. They are principally drawn by mules, seven days being the average time to Denver.

The Pony Express is a comparatively new institution, conveying letters and dispatches from St. Joseph to California, a distance of fifteen hundred miles in less than seven days. We have frequently seen this express on the road, the pony on the full run and wet with perspiration.

As we journeyed on from our last encampment, we fell in company with a Mr. R____ and wife, who had a company of eighteen persons, whom they were boarding through to Denver. We reached Gilman's Ranche, distant some seventeen miles from Smith's, where we instituted inquiries regarding wood and were told that there was no wood to be had on the river for

Letter VI

many miles. Some of us had noticed timber a few miles distant, but not knowing whether it was situated on this side of the river or on an island, we asked the question. There was a large load of cedar wood standing near that had just been hauled from the bluffs, and the company purchased a few sticks, paying at a rate of two shillings per stick. While negotiating, Mr. R____ jokingly remarked that he had a sufficient company to draw that load off. An employee of the ranche standing near, who probably was not accustomed to taking things in the "Pickwickian sense," immediately bristled up and said –

"No, I be d____d if you have. If you think you have, I would just like to see you at it."

"Well, I have," says Mr. R____, "but I did not wish it understood that I intended to take it without consent."

"Well, stranger," says the man, "it won't do to talk so in this country, remember you are not in the States."

This sentiment aroused the feelings of the company, some of whom spoke in no flattering terms of the man's character. After some little bantering, he proceeded into the house and soon emerged with a revolver, thinking, no doubt, to frighten the pilgrims.

"My friend," said one of our party, "do you intend using that? I hardly think it would be healthy for you; we are a pretty strong party and well armed."

"Well, I believe I could pick off some of you before you had much chance," spoke the fellow.

"You'd better try it on, and we'll annihilate you and this shanty," said some of the party whose looks and actions were so threatening that the fellow finally wilted and sloped back under cover, and we started on and encamped about a mile and half beyond, where we found plenty of good wood, thus proving the fellow a liar as well as a coward. Some of the party had a mind to go back and make an example of the chap but were at length persuaded from the inglorious undertaking.

As they neared the Rocky Mountains, the land grew more barren and the emigrants had to make sure their stock didn't get "alkali poisoning."
Harper's Weekly.

LETTER VII

FOX'S RANCHE—COTTONWOOD SPRINGS—
ROBBERS—HORSE STEALING, ETC.—JACK
MORROW'S—APPEARANCE OF THE BLUFFS—
MEET INDIANS TRAVELING—CHEYENNE
ENCAMPMENT—FREMONT'S SLOUGH AND
FREMONT'S SPRINGS—O'FALLON'S BLUFFS AND
U.S. MAIL STATION—MORE INDIANS—TRAVELING
AT NIGHT—NO WOOD AND FEW BUFFALO CHIPS.

Proceeding on from Gilman's, we soon reach a station known as Fox's Springs. The proprietor has, since we first passed through, vacated the premises and left for parts unknown, and there is now an opening for some enterprising man, who likes the business—any man who has had experience in horse stealing, etc., has all the qualifications necessary. There is a deep ravine a few rods beyond the ranche, and the bed of a stream (the banks of which are high and precipitous). These channels that the surging water had once dug in its course to the river are frequently met and have to be crossed; in some cases, they have been bridged, especially those whose banks are steep and rugged, and where it is thought that the traveler had rather pay twenty-five or fifty cents to cross on the bridge than descend the high banks and run the risk of injuring his team and breaking the wagon.

Passing on from this point, the next station reached is Cottonwood Springs, where there are several ranches together with a blacksmith's shop, before reaching which we have to cross another deep gully, where there are some pools of standing water and a good spring. The intervening road between these two points traverses the upper prairie, and the river banks are high. As we pass along, many prairie dog towns are noticed, which are more or less interesting to the traveler. These towns are variable in extent, sometimes covering only a few acres and others covering the surface for miles. They are composed of small mounds, conical in shape, built up sometimes to the height of two feet; others are merely slight oval elevations, having an opening either placed at the top or on the side, the whole mound being beaten down, especially on the top, which presents a hard, smooth surface. The passage into the mound descends vertically to the extent of a foot or more and then turns off obliquely. The marmots, or dogs as they are termed, who inhabit them resemble a small bull dog in appearance, are of a sandy color, and are generally seen sitting near the entrance of their house or sometimes running back and forth on visits to their neighbors.

When disturbed they always assume the erect posture, look around for a minute or more, and proceed on to their home, where they again assume the erect position. If you approach nearer, they give a series of sharp barks, and flapping their short tails, descend into the mound. They are very timid, though at times we have approached within a few rods of them. When shot while sitting near their holes they invariably fall in, and the hunter seldom secures them. It is thought by some that they have underground communications, but this is an erroneous idea—the passages to their houses terminate in a small chamber, lined with grass, where they hibernate during the winter. I have often seen several enter at one passage, but whether they all occupied it or not as a home is more than I can say. Some tell us that the marmot shares his home with a small owl and snakes, but I cannot believe it. That snakes do sometimes seek refuge there is beyond doubt. The small burrowing owl (*strix cunicularia*), generally inhabits the vacant mounds. These owls are often seen flying around the town, often settling down on the top of a mound, and when disturbed (they are very timid) they fly off, giving vent to a cry similar to that made by the dog.

This country is infested with bands of thieves and robbers, whose sole business is to stampede and secure the emigrant's stock. Along some portions of the route, constant vigilance has to be exercised. Suspicious looking characters have often been seen lurking around the camp at night in the endeavor to secure the horses or mules lassoed out; and when so seen they are often fired upon, as the emigrant has no mercy on these villains. I was told of one circumstance where a man was seen slyly creeping over the bluffs; the company were awakened by the watchman, and they decided to await and see what the fellow's intention was, as his movements could be perfectly seen, it being a bright, star-light night. He slowly and cautiously moved forward, creeping on his hands and knees in the direction of the horses, one of which, noticing the approaching object, began to snort and circle around; and the company, fearing that the animal might break loose, started out. One of their number having a gun loaded with buck-shot, sent the contents after the prowler, who was seen to fall over. Then procuring a lantern, they started out to see who it was but on reaching the spot, the "bird had flown." He had been taken off by his comrades, but whether dead or alive was unknown; the bloodstains remaining, however, were evidence that the shot had taken effect. These ruffians have their rendezvous amid the bluffs, where they hide the stock taken, and undoubtedly they have their connection with various ranches.

There is perhaps no point wherein the emigrant is more sensitive than regarding the safety of his stock, and he anxiously watches them. It is, indeed, dangerous even to go amid another man's property while searching for your own without first informing their owner. I remember at one time, while driving our cattle from an island in the river where they had been turned to feed into camp that one was overlooked, and a search was soon after made for it, and noticing one that looked like ours, and which proved to be, amid another herd, one of the party started back after it. It so happened that there were several in the herd of the same color, and our friend mistook the wrong one and was driving it over, when several of the party who owned them came running out much excited, wanting to know what the h_ll we were doing with that ox. We told them that it was ours, as we supposed it to be in the distance; but they denied it, and some hard words passed, and exclamations of "shoot the cuss!" went round. However, the matter was amicably settled as soon as the mistake on our part was apparent.

Jack Morrow's is the second station, after leaving Cottonwood Springs, there being one intervening, known as Box Elder. Morrow's Ranche, now called the Junction House, is one of the best stations on the road and is a considerable trading post with the Indians—there being a general assortment of goods kept—in fact, it is a "store." The building is composed of square cedar timbers well put up. On one side is the old building, constructed of rough logs; while on the opposite side of the road is a good corral, its walls built of hewn cedar posts. There is a good well of water. Jack Morrow is a somewhat noted character, having lived in the country many years, and has been employed by government, to some extent, in carrying the mail through to Fort Laramie and other points at a time when the Indians were hostile to the government. He is a small, slim person, rather below the average stature, light complexion, wearing long auburn hair, his features small but regular, no beard, and withal, a very social man. He had a squaw wife and has had several. By some it was thought that he was connected with the organized band of thieves, for if any one mentioned that they had lost animals, he would offer to find them for certain remuneration. We did not see him when passing back from Denver, and the *ipse dixit* (popular belief) was that he had been lynched by a party of emigrants, who had found their lost stock with him. I cannot, however, vouch for the truth of the assertion.

There is another deep ravine just beyond the house, which is bridged and no charge made for crossing it. The bluffs in the vicinity are very broken, rising up in innumerable peaks, and assuming the proportions of mountains. They are perfectly barren, except now and then a growth of cedar is seen, darkly shading their canyons, and sometimes these channels abound with a thick growth of buffalo grass and we sometimes meet with a plant known as "soap weed," or, as it is called by some, the "Mexican Dagger Plant." It is used by the Indians in washing the paint from their faces. The root is large and from its upper periphery grows a series of dagger-like blades, having a sharp, pointed extremity, which is spread out like a fan, enveloping its whole circumference. From the center of the root rises a tall spike, reaching a height of from one to two feet and having concentric whorls of white blossoms that exhale a very pleasant perfume.

Passing on from the Junction House, we continue our way across the upland, some ways from the river, a distance of eleven miles, when we again descend to the river bottom, reaching Fremont's Slough, where there is a stage station known as Bishop's Station. During the day, we met a band of migrating Indians, who were removing their effects to another locality. Their method of traveling is decidedly unique, each family going independent by itself, and I have often seen them scattered for miles over the prairie. They have generally a large number of ponies and mules, some of which bear packs and drag their lodge poles, while others are ridden by the squaws and young Indians; but few of the warriors are seen at these times, none but the decrepit old Indians and a few braves accompanying the squaws. Several ponies are called into requisition for the conveyance of their camp furniture and provisions—on one is strapped the folded covering of the lodge to each side of which is secured one extremity of two, three, and sometimes four lodge poles, the other extremities trailing out behind; at the middle is often placed an oval framework, looking like a cage, and sometimes covered with a brilliant figured calico or a blanket to screen the occupants from the sun—these occupants are the papooses or a litter of pups—and sometimes a squaw may be seen curled up within its small area, taking her siesta. The other ponies carry the various other trappings and provisions. They are always accompanied by a large number of wolfish looking dogs, to the larger of which is secured a set of smaller poles and a small pack.

While passing them, mutual salutations of "How!," "How!" were exchanged, and many of the Indians would stop and want to trade for some article of our apparel. Many of them are very proud and haughty in their bearing, considering themselves much superior to "Pale-face," who is seen drudging along like their squaws.

Their taste evinced in the matter of dress is peculiar, and we have often been amused at seeing a stalwart Indian with a blue military coat on, adorned with innumerable brass buttons, and buttoned up to the chin in the hottest days, while his lower limbs are entirely destitute of covering. Many of them are seen wearing fancy colored shirts, gaudy vests, and old felt hats; and one, I remember, had an umbrella which he carried spread above his head, which he considered as adding much to the dignity of his appearance. They all wear more or less trinkets, such as coils of brass wire and bands of silver on their arms and fingers, together with a long string of circular pieces of silver graduated in size and attached to a leather strap, which is attached and suspended from the black hair like a queue. They term it "money," and its length is generally proportionate to their wealth. Their clubs, lances and bows are often thickly studded with brass nails, which are considered very ornamental; and many of them wear looking glasses suspended around their necks.

The old squaws are very slovenly in appearance, wearing a loose cotton tunic, belted at the waist with a broad leather belt studded with large brass buttons, which is bedaubed with grease and dirt. Their faces are corrugated with wrinkles, and their hair hangs disheveled and matted about it—the abode of "creeping things," and the only method used for their eradication is picking them out with the fingers and eating them. This operation I have frequently noticed; sometimes a young squaw performs the service, cracking them between her teeth with a decided gusto.

The young squaws are neater in appearance, wearing broadcloth skirts, fancy colored blankets, bead-trimmed leggings and moccasins, and sometimes an ornamented buckskin cape. The majority of them ride when traveling either in the cage on the poles or on horseback, *a la califourchon* (astride or straddling) —sometimes with a papoose in their arms and leading or driving their pack animals.

Before reaching Fremont Slough, we passed a small encampment of Cheyenne, who are another large unsettled tribe that roam over the plains. They are the allies of the Sioux and are often seen together, frequently uniting to fight the Pawnees against whom unceasing war is waged; and it is this constant spirit of aggression and retaliation that keeps them from that apathetic and debasing state that characterizes some tribes among the mountains, who live amid the rocks and caves, subsisting on roots and any chance thing that comes within reach. The Cheyenne are tall in stature, having very fair and regular features. They are, however, abominably lazy and sometimes disgustingly filthy.

Passing on from Fremont's Slough along the river bottom, we soon reach Fremont's Springs, where there is a ranche, just beyond which the road ascends and crosses the bluffs and finally traverses a high ridge that presents a hard, even surface, covered with a short, stunted grass and in some places with large fields of "Prickly Pear." The country is sterile; and, in fact, the whole of this country beyond the 98th meridian has few features that are interesting, and some portions of it remind one of the "Arabian Desert." Its surface is seldom watered by rains; the soil is poor, consisting of granitic sand with a mixture of clay. The incinerated products of vegetation and a thick incrustation of alkali may be often seen dotting the ground, which is so hard baked and destitute of moisture that it is fissured and cracked in many places. It is a country so unsuited to the purposes of agriculture that it will never be settled, at least in our day and generation.

Bob Williams' Ranche is the next station met with, lying at the foot of O'Fallon's Bluffs on the river bottom. Two miles further travel brings us to the U. S. Mail Station, by some termed Moore & Grime's Trading Post. The Post Office that was located here has since been removed to the "Upper Crossing." On reaching this place we encamped to spend the Sabbath, turning down to the river bank where there is good camping ground and some wood; but there is none but river water to be had, which is a vile compound, very turbid and mixed with sparkling fragments of mica; and during the sultry days its taste was almost nauseous. The emigrant, however, gets used to it and considers it a great luxury in comparison to the slough water, which he is often compelled to drink, and which sloughs are the abodes of innumerable turtles, tadpoles and snakes.

Beyond us at the distance of a mile was a small encampment of Sioux Indians, and during our stay here we received frequent visits from them, which were anything but agreeable. They would come and sit down around our tent *sans ceremonie* (without ceremony), produce their pipe, light it and commence smoking, each taking a whiff or two and then passing it around to the others—while the young boys would saunter around camp, poking their dirty digitals and noses into the pots and kettles, looking for something to eat, and we had to keep a strict watch over their movements for they are great pilferers. The older Indians would frequently come up leading their smoky looking progeny and say, "Me papoose hungry!" and motion for something to eat. When anything is placed before them, they each begin to snatch, to see which will get the most, and it is amusing to see how expert they are at the business. When smoking, they suck in the exhilarating vapor, drawing it into the lungs, the expiration sending it through the nose. Their tobacco is very mild, being mixed with the dry leaves of the *salix langifolia.*

Sunday afternoon the warriors started out on a war expedition against the Pawnees, each well mounted on a pony, and many of them leading extra ones, in case one should give out, as they often do, for the peculiar construction of the saddle cuts and galls their backs, rendering them unfit to ride. The bridles are covered with plates of silver and tin, which are kept burnished as bright as a new dollar, and feathers are often affixed to the tail and mane of the pony. The faces of the braves were variously painted—some red, green, yellow, and some who were in mourning-black; and they were variously dressed—some wore hats either of straw or felt, decked with feathers, wolf tails and long streamers of ribbons, with either an old vest or coat on that had been given them by some of the emigrants; but the majority wore no head covering and nothing but their blankets wrapped around them. Their arms consisted of bows and arrows, tomahawks, clubs, a long sword lance, scalping knife, and now and then one had an old flintlock gun, and one I noticed had a revolver. On asking one where he was going, says he, "Ugh! Me big Injun, kill heap Pawnee—so, so!" motioning how he did it; and then, for his condescension in telling me held out his hand wanting "whisk, tobac," etc. They always mount their horse on the off side, putting the right foot in the stirrup and throwing the left over the saddle, which looks very awkward; the squaws, however, mount on the opposite side.

While at this point, we learned that we should find no more wood for a distance of one hundred and seventy miles, so we turned our attention to cooking, baking bread, making pies, etc.; but as our convenience for carrying such provender was very indifferent, we did not cook as much as we otherwise should, but before leaving we took aboard all the wood that we could make room for. The third day out, bread, pies, and wood were gone, and buffalo chips were few and far between, and those found were decidedly thin in consistence, and some rather fresh.

Before reaching this station, a week or so previous, a terrific storm of wind and hail had swept over this locality, stampeding the emigrants' stock and doing damage to their tents and wagons; and such a degree of cold was induced that several, while hunting for their stock, were benumbed and froze to death and were buried near this ranche. Their graves were situated just back of a little rise of ground below the bluffs.

After leaving the U.S. Mail Station, we again leave the river bottom and traverse the upper prairie, there being a strip of

Letter VII

sand to cross before reaching the high land. During the day, a fierce storm of wind sprung up from the north that threatened to wreck us, but a drizzly rain setting in abated its violence somewhat, and we continued on to the Express Station, a distance of sixteen miles. We reached this station wet, cold and covered with mud, for clouds of sand and dirt had swept over us, adhering to the wet surface of our garments. We turned into camp here, but the wind continued to blow a gale, and we could neither erect the tent nor cook supper, but taking a cold bite, retired to our wagon to pass the night, and it passed miserably. The morning brought no cessation of the storm, but we managed to get a fire after much trouble and made some coffee, which somewhat revived our drooping spirits, and we pressed on, shivering and quaking with the extreme cold. The storm finally abated at noon, and we welcomed the return of "better weather" with grateful emotions.

LETTER VIII

LONE TREE RANCHE—FEED SCARCE—LOWER CROSSING—UPPER CROSSING—SAND HILLS AND GRAVEL PITS—LILLIAN SPRINGS—OUR GLEE CLUB—MORE SAND AND A STORM—CATTLE AND CATTLE DRIVING—BEAVER CREEK, AND FIRST SIGHT OF THE MOUNTAINS—BOATING ON THE PLATTE.

The next station reached is the "Lone Star Ranche," situated near the borders of the river and kept by two Frenchmen named Geroux and Dion. It was here, on our return, that a sad accident occurred, a result of too frequent intercourse with the Indian in the matter of trading. A man accompanied by his wife was returning to the States; on reaching this point where some Indians were encamped, his attention was directed to a noble mule in the possession of one of them, and he wished to buy it. The Indian manifested a willingness to sell and on being asked the price, spread out the fingers of both hands, closed them, and then spread them again, signifying that he wanted twenty dollars. The man counted out the sum of twenty half dollars and gave it into the hand of the Indian, who looked at it, counted it over and over, and finally, shaking his head, returned it back. The man who had considered the bargain as made, supposing the Indian to mean half dollars, which is their general standard of counting, was provoked at him for handing it back, and perhaps incensed to think the Indian had so just an appreciation of the animal's value, turned and struck him. This was an unpardonable offense; an Indian would rather be killed than suffer such an indignity. He turned, muttering revenge, which is the breath of the Indian's life, and went to his lodge, got his bow and quiver, mounted his pony and returned. The man, seeing the intent of the Indian, took refuge in his wagon and started on. The Indian encircled the wagon and soon sent an arrow into it, which had no other effect than to badly frighten the woman, who immediately jumped from it to the ground; as she did so, another arrow sped like the wind from the heavy bow, piercing her side and passing through the liver. The Indian was then satisfied, his vengeance was appeased, and he returned to his encampment. The woman was taken up and carried into the ranche, where the arrow was extracted. We reached the place on the following day, but the man and his suffering wife had gone ahead; we met them, however, at the U.S. Mail Station; she was comfortable and was likely to recover.

Many of the emigrants, while passing over the road, had an eye to a sharp bargain with the Indians in obtaining furs, buffalo skins and ponies; and, more or less, trouble was the frequent result. All their old guns, oiled and brightened up, were offered in trade for a pony and provided the trade was consummated, they had to watch them close, for the Indian often followed them to steal them; if unsuccessful, he will come out openly and want you to trade back. Many of the travelers bought buffalo skins for a cup or two of sugar, and I have known them to walk a mile or two in order to affect such a trade. Many, in direct opposition to the commands of government, would exchange fire-arms, ammunition and whisky for furs, skins, etc., and it was surprising that much more trouble did not occur than did, owing to the strong desire for wealth of the traveler.

As we passed on we found feed very scarce; it had been most miserable since we first entered upon the journey, the grass being short and stunted, and especially upon the high prairie it was much withered and burnt, but now the quantity as well as the quality was growing "beautifully less," and the poor animals suffered. They were becoming thin; the outlines of their ribs standing out more and more sharp every day, and the inter-osseous spaces sinking deeper. What was to be done? Echo sadly answered, "What!" The cattle could not labor long on poor feed; as it was, their animal courage was fast ebbing, although the driver's whip and goad was constantly exercised in stimulating it. We fed them on small rations of corn, so long as it lasted, and now and then drove them down upon the river bottom, where by traversing over a large extent of surface they could at times get a fill, but it was generally hazardous to turn them out upon some of the bottoms for the reason of there being such abundance of alkali, not only scattered in thick incrustations over the surface but impregnating the water and grass; and did they drink of the water or eat of the grass, they were certain of being more or less injured, and many times have died from its effects. It destroys and disorganizes the mucous coating of the stomach and intestines, stimulates the kidneys, etc. When an animal is known to be thus poisoned, vinegar is often administered in order to neutralize it and sometimes with most happy effects. Some introduce a piece of fat bacon into their stomach, but a better method is to mix a portion of oil with corn meal and feed it. This (the oil) chemically united with the alkali, forming a compound that is inert and passes off with the final result of digestion.

During the day, our monotonous tramp was brought to a sudden halt by the exclamation that a lot of chickens had escaped the coop; and sure enough, the late well-housed domestic brood was abroad, strutting around with the freedom they so much envied of their prairie neighbors. All hands were soon in action to again secure them and such running and dodging, flying and jumping, I doubt was ever before seen on the plains. Now we thought we had them then presto, we didn't have 'em, a feather or two being the only trophy of the grip; but after some time spent by the company in the chase with whips and sticks, all of the fugitives were captured; three, however, had fallen victim to the heavy blows of their angry pursuers and lay in *articulo mortis* (at the point of death) upon the plain.

We soon reached the lower, or "Old California Crossing" as it is called, where there are two ranches and a blacksmith's shop, and there was also a small encampment of Indians there at the time we passed. The emigration to California used to cross the river at this point, but now the majority crosses twenty-two miles above.

Passing on from this point, we encountered a great many "Stampeders," who were happy in knowing that they were soon to experience

> *"Those throbs of sweet delight,*
>
> *That lives when native scenery meets the sight,"*

and they passed us, bestowing many a pitying glance; and we, in turn, looked contemptuously at them, meantime asking if they were going home to see their "mammas." "Yes, and you'll be glad to see the 'maternal apron string' before you get to the mountains" was the reply. Some told us that the Peak had "broken off, and added, "that ar quartz mill of your is no account, 'twont sell for old iron."

During the drive, we passed vast quantities of *artemesia,* wild sage or prairie sage, as it is variously called, the under surface of its leaves glistening like silver when turned up by the breeze; and we also noticed a great many small rose bushes, reminding us of home and civilization. They were very dwarfish in size, bearing roses of various colors and were very fragrant. The road at times led through deep ravines and gravel pits and occasionally over a piece of sand, which was deep and heavy, and often times it was necessary to "double up" our teams in order to pull our heavy loads across. At length we reached the "Upper Crossing," where there is a little cluster of framed buildings together with a good well of water, which to us was a gratifying sight, and we hastened with kegs, canteens and buckets for a supply. This point is the headquarters of Beaubien, the old Indian trader. We saw him here, seated in the store, surrounded by several stout warriors, passing the pipe and telling stories.

Leaving the place, the road traverses over some heavy sand hills that border on the river and it required no mean exertion to cross them. We had to double up, putting four and six yoke to a wagon, and then the lungs of a Stentor (an extremely loud person) and the arms of Briareus (a Greek 100-arm monster) were wanted to yell at the cattle and push and lift at the wheels. These sand drifts strike terror to the hearts of the emigrants and call for an extra exertion from the team; and during a hot day, when the solar rays fall and are reflected from the sands with a scorching heat; when the air comes to your lungs with a suffocating dryness, as from an oven, expanding the fluids of the system until every channel seems ready to burst; when the cattle give out every few rods and stand lolling and blowing, seeming ready to melt; then it is hard—it is terrible. Many such days did we experience; and in crossing a long strip of sand, the under currents of a man's nature begins to work, throwing up the sediments, and many have I heard curse and damn the country and everything in it until satisfied they could not do the matter justice and then quit, seemingly much relieved after so free an expenditure of hot air. These sand beds vary in extent—some of them do not exceed one-half mile in length, while others stretch out for miles. In crossing it, we found it necessary to halt every few minutes in order to rest the cattle that they might not give out, which is not infrequently the case

Letter VIII

as the many carcasses of horses and cattle evince, and which are seen lying in and behind the road. In fact, the Platte Valley is more or less covered with the putrescent rotting remains of many poor animals, the victims of alkali, over-work, and the driver's abuse; and the bleaching fragments of skeletons may be seen everywhere, as they have been scattered o'er the plain by the prowling and insatiate wolf; and there they lie, the mute though eloquent preachers of a much needed reform in the matter of traveling and driving stock across the wide wastes of the Western world.

Thirty miles farther travel over the high prairie and along the river bottom, alternating from one to the other, brings us to Lillian Springs, where there is an adobe building occupied as a trading post; and there is also one of the best springs of water that is to be met with on the whole line of travel. We encamped at this point Saturday night and remained over Sunday. While there we instituted what we termed "our glee club" for the purpose of promoting our own and the happiness of others, all of which was the result of finding an old copy of the "Dime Song Book."

On Sabbath eve the spirit of song was evoked, and we gave our first concert to the breezes in the Temple of Nature, accompanied by the "fine pause of evening" and the "voice of gentle zephyrs," and with no other instruments save those attuned by Deity. The supply of gas which usually illuminated the camp failed, and we resorted to a "star candle" on this particular occasion, to enable us to see the words of the songs in the accumulating darkness. The concert opened with a performance by the "Germania Band," consisting of two Teutons, who at the time were engaged in washing and wiping the metallic supper dishes, and the click and clatter of the plates and the jingle of knives and forks added fine effect to their song of "*Den lieben langen tag,*" which was considered a "decided hit" and was encored with prolonged shouts of B*ravo! Bravissimo!* Then followed the pathetic song of "Home, sweet home" by the company, sung *con animo* (with spirit or intention), and then a few of the lively negro melodies were called for, accompanied by "sympathetic pedal variations," then the spirited and soul-stirring songs of "The Star Spangled Banner" and "Red, White and Blue" were sung; and finally the familiar and time-tested "Old Lang Syne" was sent out, every note lifted *forte* (strongly), then *fortissimo,* until the echoes of "time past" awoke our "old acquaintance," and we retired to look back into the vista of time and travel, and to think of the loved ones at home.

Our music, like that of the fabled Orpheus (the Greek mythological "Father of Song"), did not tame the beasts of the desert nor did it cause the stones of our projected city to rise and form themselves into stately buildings, like that of Amphion; but it unloosed the burdens of care, and we rose to the full dignity of men once more and pursued our journey with better spirits and brighter hopes.

Leaving Lillian Springs, more sand hills and gravel pits have to be crossed, and then we traverse the river bottom again for a few miles, when we again reach another very heavy piece of sand that looms up discouragingly; the wagon wheels were buried in it to the depth of eight and ten inches, and it was all that six yoke of cattle could do to drag a wagon through.

During the day we passed a large encampment of Sioux Indians and were visited at noon by "Thimka-wam-pa-li," or Long Chin, dressed *a la militaire* (in the military style), having a heavy old-fashioned sword hung around his neck and bringing a "begging paper" and the daguerreotypes (photos) of himself and squaw in his hands. He was accompanied by his papoose, who also carried a small sword, and an old pistol with a cartridge

Letter VIII

box belted around his waist. He stated that he had been "way off to Washington, saw heap white man, who "shakee" hand, say "How! Howdy do!" and shaking our hands. We made him some presents, before starting out, of sugar, tobacco, etc., which were received with expression of "good!" and "How-dy-do! sah!.," which were eminently gratifying.

Passing on we soon encountered more sand, and while in the midst of it, a heavy gale of wind broke over us, a perfect tornado, filling the air with clouds of sand; and so suddenly did it come upon us that we had barely time to "'bout ship" before it struck us, stripping off our wagon sheets and scattering the light surface articles of the load. It lasted for the space of twenty minutes and then abated, when we passed on. Our cattle, at this stage of the journey, became tender footed to some extent and often took fits of crowding and hauling, which were very annoying. We could sometimes remedy this by tying their heads together but more frequently had to stop and change sides with them. Some of the cattle were so used up that they could not work and were driven along behind the train. At last they were sold to a Ranchero for a small consideration.

Cattle were many times sadly abused, being whipped, pounded, kicked and goaded unmercifully; and I have often seen raw and bleeding surfaces, the result of strokes continually applied at one spot, and the animal would cringe and quiver at every cut. Drivers would often mount the wagon and ride, and the wearied team taking advantage of their absence, would flag in pace and sometimes turn from the road. As soon as the driver's attention was called to their slow motions, with a curse he would dismount, and running up to the leaders, lay on the gad until he had the team under full trot, when he would again get up on the wagon and wait for another opportunity to settle "old scores."

The names of the cattle were peculiar, and we were often amused at hearing them drawled out by the drivers, when encouraging them on to travel. It was "Get up! Rum and Brandy." "Roll up there, Douglas, you black scoundrel you!" "G'lang! Sandy, Duke, Prince, Jim, John, etc., etc.," and one old chap who was driving three yoke of cattle always spoke of them as his "beloved Christian brethren." He said that before starting they belonged to several denominations, but they had lately been immersed and were now all Baptists, except one old sinner there on the wheel, who was "a little doubtful, yet had an idea that "he'd come under conviction by the time he got through."

After traveling a distance of twenty-three miles, we reached Valley Station, which is located near the river. The stage company has a station there. On leaving here we cross a small strip of sand, then the road traverses the upper prairie, which is hard and level, with now and then a deep ravine to cross; and twenty-seven miles farther on brings us to Beaver Creek, where are the ruins of two sod houses. It was here that we caught

When the Rocky Mountains were spotted, everyone was always a lot less tired. The end of the journey was literally in sight.
Ludlow, *The Heart of the Continent.*

Letter VIII

our first view of the mountains. The outlines, however, of the two peaks (one of which was "Long's") that were visible were so dim and cloud-like that many had their doubts concerning them; and it was not until we had proceeded some miles further on that our doubts gave way, and the cry of "The mountains! The mountains!" was shouted from one end of the train to the other. Each team was stopped, and a reserved demijohn of "pure Bourbon" that had been hid away in the boiler was produced and congratulations were exchanged *ad infinitum.* Soon the whole chain of mountains was visible, looking like a group of heavy clouds belting the horizon. The sight was pleasing, for we could now see the end and aim of our journey, and we experienced about the same feelings that the mariner does when "land ho!" is proclaimed from the mizzen-top after a long and stormy voyage across the main. For days and days, the dreary open plain had stretched out before us until lost to view in the sky; but now, the high snow-clad peaks and lofty ridges of the mighty mountains stood out to mark our progress, and we drove on, calculating the distance yet to be canceled. The slow motions of our cattle were now more tedious than ever, and, as one of the company happily expressed it, we were going like a "n____ funeral," notwithstanding frequent applications of whip and goad; but *"Festina Lente"* ("hasten slowly" – a saying of the Roman Emperor Augustus) is and ever must be the motto of those who travel across the plains with no other conveyance than that of a heavily loaded wagon drawn by stags, steers and cows.

While encamped on Beaver Creek in the latter part of August, we notice several parties passing down the river in boats of a scow shape and built of rough pine boards; but their progress was often interrupted by striking the sand bars, when their craft would swing round and stop, then the boatmen would have to get out and drag it over, which was effected after much delay, by tugging at the bow-line and pushing at the stern. The sand bars are very wide and numerous in many places, and a great effort was required to cross them; and the majority who attempted to navigate the Platte at this season, after proceeding down a hundred miles or so, left their boats and took to the road.

LETTER IX

THE CUT-OFF—BIJOU CREEK—SOMETHING CONCERNING THE ALKALI—FREMONT'S ORCHARD AND FREMONT'S HILL—GETTING FOOT-SORE—BUFFALO BIRDS—AN OBJECT OF CHARITY—MORE ABOUT THE ROAD AND COUNTRY—ARRAPAHOE INDIANS—NEAR OUR JOURNEY'S END—DENVER CITY ALL ABOUT DENVER—EXECUTION OF A MURDERER, ETC.

Leaving Beaver Creek, we follow along the upper prairie some distance back from the river for a distance of ten or twelve miles, where we again descend to the bottom road, having a small strip of sand to cross; we then follow up the bottom for some seven miles and again ascend to the high land, where there is a stage station, and two miles beyond this we reach a branch road leading to Denver and known as the "Cut-Off." This road was surveyed at the expense of Majors, Russel & Co. and is traveled by their stages. It is the most direct road to Denver City, saving some forty miles of travel; but there was a general distrust of it last spring, and many were the stories told regarding it—some saying that there was no water and but little grass to be had and that it was lined with the carcasses of dead bullocks; and some person had written on the stump of a pole standing there, "Gentlemen and ladies will please go the old road; d__d fools will take the cut-off." Others stated that it was a good road, there being plenty of water and grass, and withal free from sand. This latter statement concerning the road is,

A Trip To Pike's Peak & Notes By The Way

An Arapaho village on the Platte River just a short distance from the new white settlement of Denver.
Richardson, *Beyond the Mississippi.*

in many respects, true and should I ever repeat the journey, I would give this new road the preference, for it cannot have any worse features than those possessed by the old road, since most of the sand that we encountered on the whole route is located between this point and Denver.

After leaving the cut-off, there is a long strip of heavy sand to cross, which extends to Bijou Creek, a small clear running stream, but which is more or less tinctured with alkali; and it was generally considered unsafe to allow the cattle to drink of it. This alkali consists of potash, soda, lime, magnesia, etc., the products of burnt grass and plants, which have been consumed by the fires that often sweep over these vast prairies. We frequently saw large surfaces thickly incrusted with it, and so thick was the deposit that we could have scraped up bushels of it. It is more frequently observed after a heavy rain, it being dissolved and then precipitated upon the surface of the ground.

Passing on from this creek, we found near the river bank a fine spring of water issuing from a crevice in the wall rock, falling into a moss lined basin and passing through a pebbly channel to the river—one of those crystal founts whose beauty is fully as refreshing as its water. After some miles of travel over the upland, we descended and encamped for the night on a beautiful bottom, where we found excellent feed for our stock. After supper, and while many of us were seated within the tent engaged at euchre, several of our number without discovered what they termed an *ignis fatuus* (will-o-wisp) dancing over the bottom near a line of marsh, and all were called out to look at it; when followed some learned discussions concerning its cause, character, etc., some relating incidents regarding it, how it had often misled the traveler, turning him from the road and leading him over swamp and morass; and Fred (one of our German friends) said that he had seen "more as one" in the "fader-land" and was eager to go and examine into this. Just then, another one appeared, moving backwards and forwards and apparently approaching us, and several of the party with Fred at the head proceeded after it. After some minutes they returned and stated that they had succeeded in getting quite close to it, and one remarked that it was the "prettiest thing he ever saw, burning with a blue, flickering flame"—"owing to its gaseous nature," interrupted one, "and it has a sulphurous kind of smell." "Yes, it schmells like the tyfel," spoke Fred. All were eager that we should go and see for ourselves. Some of us had our boots off, but wishing to get a nearer view of the phenomenon, were putting them on and were about ready to start, when a smothered, tell-tale snicker from one of the party arrested our attention, and we decided to remain status quo and await the *denouement* ("untying" – usually used as a literary critical term). Our friends, seeing that we were determined, frankly admitted that we had been "sold," and that our will-'o-the-wisps were two lanterns in the hands of men, who were out looking up their cattle. It is unnecessary to state that many a merry peal of laughter rang through camp when the sequel of their tramp over the bogs was known.

On leaving here, we follow up the bottom and soon rise a heavy hill, which leads us over a ridge for a distance of about two miles, when we descend a precipitous bank and find ourselves in Fremont's Orchard, where there are many ancient looking cottonwoods bearing a striking resemblance to so many old apple trees, which is the first timber that is met with after leaving O'Fallon's bluff. The bluffs or the sand hills that border this orchard on one side are cut and divided into many channels, which wind and circle back for long distances, sometimes terminating abruptly but more often dividing into others, which if followed, will sometimes lead to the summit of the hill or back again to the bottom from whence we started. In following them up, we notice on either side many niches and caves together with isolated pillars and columns of sand; indeed, in many places it is like groping through the ruins of an ancient city. Here is an old cathedral front with its gothic arches and columns, its pinnacles and spires, its ornamented niches and canopies, and large ramified windows; and there are numerous pedestals, towers and fantastic figures, all of which are exceedingly curious and well worthy of more than a passing notice.

We continued our way through the orchard, which stretches out for a half mile or more; and at a distance of four miles reached Fremont's Hill, which is decidedly a "hill of difficulty." Here we had to put four, six, and eight yoke of cattle to a wagon, and then it was amazing hard work to climb it, for it is very high and steep, and the road up it being much cut up, the wagon wheels sinking deeply in the sand. After reaching the summit, we follow over a sandy ridge for a mile, when we descend to a marshy bottom, where if some care is not exercised in driving, your whole establishment gets stalled. We encamped on this bottom, having accomplished a distance of only ten miles with a vast amount of labor and anxiety. While passing over this hill, we had a magnificent view of the mountains that somewhat calmed our perturbed spirits; and then before us lay a landscape of surpassing beauty, diversified with hill, dale, and plain, through which could be seen the broad and glimmering waters of the Platte with its many islands and timber-lined banks and bayous.

Many of us were getting foot-sore, for of late we had been compelled to walk in order to relieve the jaded teams, and we exchanged our heavy boots for moccasins, which were far more comfortable to the feet. Many have I seen so lame that it was almost impossible to walk; huge blisters would form on the heels, would break, and the friction on their heavy boots would soon tear off the cuticle leaving a festering sore. Others, again, who possessed a rheumatic diathesis (heat under the skin), would often awake in the morning with rigid and sore muscles, scarcely able to walk, and they were often seen hobbling through the sand with the aid of a stick or hanging on the back end of the wagon.

On our return, we met one old fellow badly circumstanced. We found him sitting beside the road, so overcome with heat, pain and fatigue that he could go no farther. As we approached, he asked for water, but we had nothing but a little cold coffee, which we offered, and which he hastily drank. He then informed us that he had before leaving Denver bargained for a passage to the States with a man who was to meet him at the next ranche, some five miles distant, and that he had started out to walk it but had been attacked with rheumatism and was now scarcely able to put one foot before the other and wished us to help him along, which we agreed to do and assisted him into the wagon. He stated that he had been in the mountains ever since the spring of 1859 and had, when leaving home, six hundred dollars in money; but now his money was all gone with nothing to show for it, and he did not know whether he should ever reach the States again. He had spent some time at the Cache le Poudre mines, and in Gregory's district, and finally went over to Tarryall, where he remained some time, then went to the head waters of the Arkansas; but he had been unsuccessful everywhere and was trying to get home to Vermont, where he should remain. We left him at the ranche indicated and passed on; but some days after, saw him seated upon a load of hides that some emigrant had bought up to take back to the States, and in this manner he was going home. He was an object of pity—the joints of one limb were so stiffened that he could not use them, suffering pain, teased by innumerable gnats and flies, covered with dust, and withal, the day was very sultry and large beads of perspiration were distilling from every pore and trickling down his dirt-begrimed face; yet he was patient and, to some degree cheerful and expressed himself as decidedly fortunate in securing even such a conveyance.

The bottom below Fremont's Hill extends for a distance of about five miles, when we again ascend to the high land. During our passage over it we saw vast flocks of what are termed buffalo birds, and among them were a few of the red winged black bird, or tropical. These buffalo birds are expert fly catchers and would often come and alight upon the backs of our cattle and there ride and watch for flies. They were very tame and fearless, often approaching quite close to our own persons. The birds seen upon the plains are various, aside from those mentioned in a former letter; we often saw the raven *(corvus corax)* in flocks around the remains of dead animals, croaking

Letter IX

and quarreling, and now and then hopping up to notice our approach, and finally flying off at a short distance, where they would await until we passed before returning to their feast. Several species of falcon were common, and now and then might be seen the bald eagle (*Aquila leucocephalusi*) circling and sailing high above us.

We pass over the high prairie for some distance, having a good firm road to traverse but soon descended again through a bed of heavy sand and reached a narrow bottom, where the road winds around the margin of the bluffs, whose rock-crowned summits bear the inevitable marks of time's disintegrating fingers, and huge masses had been cast loose and lay in confused heaps at their bases. While trailing through this bottom, some heavy nimbus clouds came swooping down, discharging hail that fell like grape shot around us, and driving us under cover. As soon as it abated, we turned out and encamped, but there was little peace and comfort in store for us; about midnight we were awakened to a consciousness that "little drops of water make big miseries" as well as "mighty oceans," for our bedding was just on the point of swimming. The mighty Jove was driving a furious storm, which had broken above us, deluging us with rain that was fast flooding the bottom and hurling his fiery darts abroad that hissed and crackled in their descent like so many glowing bars plunged in water. Then the hoarse and heavy thunder that rolled with a quaking motion above us so shook our "nervous centers" that we stood for a time like mummies swathed in bands of fear and doubt. Our tent had become thoroughly soaked and was dripping, every thread like so many siphons; many of us took to spouting, not at all relishing this hydropathical treatment, for our spirits and animal heat were already much reduced and had it not been for the liberal potations of "fire water" that some took, the *argentums vivum* (quicksilver) of their existence might have congealed. We ran to the wagons and got our rubber clothing as soon as there was the least abatement in the storm and then "stood it out" till morning—when the heavens cleared up, and we hung our blankets and bedding out to dry.

The country that we were then passing over was essentially the same as that which we had been traversing since leaving the U. S. Mail Station—drear, barren, and unfit for agricultural purposes, covered here and there with cacti in bloom, and a species of xapaver or poppy, together with several varieties of equisetum and short grass. Now and then, patches of earth would be seen perfectly nude, destitute of any vegetation.

Passing on from the point, where we last encamped, we soon climb upon another ridge, through a strip of sand, and follow along the high prairie for the distance of eight or ten miles and then again turn down on the bottom, which was covered with good grass that afforded a feast to the cattle.

On starting out in the morning, our German friend, whom I have before mentioned, took a hunting fit and, after cleaning his *flinte,* started off into the bluffs, telling us that he would show "more game as we never did see;" we saw no more of him until afternoon, when we caught sight of him wearily approaching, dragging a lame leg and blowing like a porpoise, his face steaming and dripping, congested with fatigue and heat, and looking like a boiled lobster with his gun swung over his shoulders and bearing in his hand a terrapin.

"*Wie geht's, Kapitan* (how are you, Captain)," said we, "*es ist einer schwere warme Tag* (it is a really warm day)?" "*Yah,*" said he, and wanted "wasser." He said that he had walked "more as thirty miles" and seen nothing but "one d__n wolf," and he "pe tam if he never went mit himself again on such a *gefahrlich* expedition." His starch had evidently been dressed out and not feeling "so wohl" as usual, he turned into the wagon

Letter IX

to rest and recuperate—leaving the terrapin, the only fruit of his day's sport, in the hands of the company.

Passing on through the river valley, we again mount to the upland and pass on to within two miles of St. Vrain's Fort, when we turn due south and follow up the river to Denver. The old road continues on to St. Vrain's and leads to the Cache le Poudre Mines, Boulder City, and other mountain districts after crossing the river, which is bridged. During the day, we had a magnificent view of the mountains, and they looked "sublimely beautiful" towards evening, when bathed in the mellow light of closing day; their sky-blue tinted bases and the darker shade of their canyons contrasting grandly with the sparkling white capped peaks of the snowy axis, producing an effect most pleasing, and one which will never be forgotten.

After turning south on the Denver road, we pass the ruins of Fort Lancaster, and farther on those of Fort Lupton, where there is a ranche. These old forts were built of blocks of sod and were quite extensive, covering nearly a half acre of ground. While at Fort Lupton, we learned that we were only twenty-five miles from Denver, which tidings were received with glad rejoicings, and we hastened on, pleased to know that our journey was so near accomplished. When within six miles of the city, we turned down upon the flats and encamped, where we turned our attention to cleaning up, preparatory to our *entree* into the metropolis of the gold region. Our smutty over-alls and shirts were cast off, the boots were brushed and oiled, and the clean shirts and collars that had been reserved for this occasion were brought out and put on; and, altogether, we made such a change in our respective toilets that each looked at the other with a wondering gaze which seemed to say, "I know you not." Indeed we scarcely knew ourselves, so familiar had we become with "ragged and dirty misery" during forty days' travel over the plains; but we soon got better acquainted with our outer man, and the next morning, feeling quite natural, started out for Denver.

We soon met with a large encampment of Arapahoe Indians, many of whom flocked around us to beg, while the children would cling and climb around our wagon to see what they could steal, and such a nuisance were they that we finally applied the lash to several, which drove them away. With them were a few Comanche and Apaches. The Arapahos are a large tribe and roam from one point to another over the plain, now and then starting out on a war expedition against the Utes, who live in and beyond the mountains. They are large in person, and many are eminently entitled to the name of *"Gros Ventre,"* (big bellied) being fashioned much like the histrionic Falstaff; others again are tall and slim. Their sole dependence, like that of the other tribes on the plains, is the buffalo, which furnishes them with coverings for their lodges, food, fuel, and clothing, and with thread, cordage, lariats for their horses and strings for their bows, with buckets for water, and with the means for obtaining what they desire from the traders. When this animal is extinct, they too must perish.

At ten o'clock on the morning of the sixth of June, we encamped on the high-land just above the city, which presented a very neat appearance, and which was far more extensive than we had conceived it to be. Our journey over the great American Desert was at last accomplished; before us were the abodes of civilization and refinement, amid which could be seen the hurrying to and fro of business, and the hum and rattle of its noisy machinery was music to our ears, telling of enterprise and industry; while to the right were the smoky wigwams of the Aborigines, amid which could be seen the dusky forms of stalwart Indians, filthy squaws and naked children, lazily basking in the warm sun-light. As we turned from the one to view the other, what a contrast was there; here were the rude huts

Letter IX

of barbarism, there the elegant abodes of civilization; here was the wild untutored savage, and there the refined and educated white man. Surely the two extremes had met here beneath the frowning peaks of the Rocky Mountains in a region of country which a few years since was unknown and not coveted, but which is now the abode of a hundred thousand active, working men, bearing aloft the torch of progress, who are exploring and delving into those huge "monuments of time" for their hidden treasures—scaling their highest pinnacles, diving down into their lowest pits, drifting in at their bases, and turning from their accustomed channels the swift running torrents that roll through their winding canyons—ever seeking for that "bright eye of the mine, that lode star of the soul"—Gold!

Denver City is situated partly upon the river bottom and partly upon the sides and summit of a sloping bluff that sets back some distance from the river and has a population of about six thousand. Many fine, large and substantial buildings are to be seen in every square, some of which are constructed of

Auraria is on the left of this drawing, while the new town of Denver is on the right. Both towns were beginning to sport some pretty substantial buildings.
Frank Leslie's Illustrated Newspaper.

brick that are manufactured in the vicinity. One wonders while passing through the various avenues at its compactness and the air of comfort and finish that is everywhere apparent. Denver now includes the town of Auraria, which portion is divided from Denver proper by a "dry run" known as Cherry Creek, which is bridged at several points. The bottom below the city is covered here and there with groves of cottonwood and affords good camping ground to the emigrant; at the time we reached there, it was covered with numerous tents and wagons, as well as the open spaces and yards above in the city.

The business transacted there is large and increasing; (wagon) trains were continually arriving, bringing provisions and goods, filling the spacious warehouses and stores; and now its market will supply all the wants of the miner and resident, furnishing not only the necessities of life, but to some extent the luxuries. Its streets were swarming with miners from the mountains and with the arriving emigrants; and the din and bustle of trade, the hurry of preparation for a start into the mountains, the roll and jar of heavy carts and wagons, and withal, the hoarse cry of the auctioneer and the calling bell of the milkman furnished a scene of activity that was pleasing to look upon.

But Denver has many features that are less pleasing. There is a pestilential taint at work in the constitution of its society, which now and then throws off humors bile, that render the lives of its citizens unsafe; and how could it be otherwise, when the society is constituted of a number of loose individuals from every part of the Union and from many portions of the world, who have flocked together with like motives; far removed from all the restraints of law and order, and many of them bloated with evil, putrid with vice, full of a villainous stench and poison that was offensive at home, and yet remains a horror and a pestilence in their present abode.

Letter IX

The Provisional Government was feeble in the protection of life and property. In fact, its organization seemed to offer a premium for crime, as murder and assassination were frequent and not only was those perpetrated under the cover of night but in the broad glare of day in the open streets. Its agents were often corrupt and vicious, and justice was rarely administered; and the usurpation of power by a clique, styling themselves the "Vigilance Committee," and their atrocious acts of midnight murder and plunder, excited an untold horror in the minds of all.

But of late, there has been an entire revolution in some matters of government, and not a few of these villains, who set God and man at defiance, have met their just reward at the hands of an outraged community.

Gambling is carried on quite extensively, there being, at the time we were there, some twelve saloons, where the various games of monte, roulette, faro, keeno, fluff, etc. were played. The two largest of these saloons were known as "Denver Hall" and the "El Dorado;" and every night would find them crowded with a miscellaneous group of humanity comprised of miners, merchants, lawyers, doctors, professional gamblers, *cum multis aliis* (with many others), all engaged, either at play or eagerly watching the fortunes of their friends. The scene was one characteristic of the country and the place. Every man's adjudicator, in the shape of revolver or dirk either hung at his side or lay upon the table, ever ready to decide difficulties. Then the recklessness and trickery of the gamesters, the excitement exhibited by the bystanders, the noise and confusion, the swearing that was continually ventilated, rising with the fumes of tobacco and bad liquor, made (with the squeaking cat-gut above in the orchestra) a striking feature of life in Denver that was heart sickening. The gates of these hells were always open and always will be,

"Until fools, to keep their money can contrive,"

but the day is so far removed that the fraternity need never fear of having now and then a goose to pluck, for there, as well as in the States, dollars and sense seldom keep company.

The amusements in Denver are various. Aside from that of gambling, which is generally the most attractive, is horse-racing, and this sport is carried on extensively. While we were there, a race for one thousand dollars a side came off, the horses carrying pound shoes on their feet. Theatrical exhibitions are sometimes offered by a strolling company, who travel through the mining districts, now and then coming into the city, and these are very well supported. There are also bowling alleys and billiard halls. In one of the latter that I visited, there were six tables, and it was furnished in every respect equal to any in the States.

A lot of Denver's citizens just lived in their wagons during the summer. Tents were a little warmer, but it took a cabin to spend the winter.
Frank Leslie's Illustrated Newspaper.

Letter IX

The miners often come down from the mountains into the town for the purpose of recreation, and I have often seen them standing around the public houses and saloons, watching and remarking upon the fresh arrivals; and one I remember, a broad, merry faced Irishman, having a crop of dirty red hair spread profusely over his face, was calling the attention of his chum to a little, slim personage, who had just come in remarking:

"An' Jim, what d'ye think he'll be after doin' wid hisself, wid his leddy fingers, hould the pick and shovel, when the little bag o' flour and the wee bit o' bacon is aiten up complately?"

"An' sure," said his companion, "won't he do like every mother's son of us—kape on digging."

"Faith, its complamenting him ye are; wid his sickly constitoshun, wouldn't he be after taking hisself back to Ameriky to his swate-heart?"

Various are the witticisms lavished on new comers, especially if they exhibit any eccentricity of dress or any physical peculiarities; and they are all not less pointed than course in their remarks, and in general they indulge in more or less careless talk that is so productive of mischief in a new country.

The old mountaineer, Kit Carson, was in Denver, at the time we reached there but to see him with his full, good natured face, and dressed in a sober suit of black, one would scarcely conceive him to be the sturdy and invincible Kit Carson, the pathfinder of the Rocky Mountains, and the terror of the Indians. We expected to find him a man with hard stern features and dressed in fringed buckskin from head to toe after the manner of most mountaineers. His home is in New Mexico, where he has the agency of the Ute Indians, receiving a salary from the government.

Before leaving the city, we witnessed the execution of a German, who had been found guilty of murder after a fair trial in the Provisional court, held beneath the shade of some large cottonwoods below the city, a rope circle marking its limits, while a carpenter's bench not only furnished a seat for the judges and a "bar" for the pleaders, but the general furniture of the court. After a trial that occupied the better part of two days, the German, who was an ignorant, uncouth specimen of his race, was found guilty of willful and premeditated murder by the three judges, and the sentence of death by hanging was considered the proper punishment; but before sentence was passed, the verdict was referred to the people for ratification, and the general acclaim was in its favor. The prisoner was then asked if he had anything to say, and he arose and addressed the people in a few unintelligible words, whereby he insisted that the act was committed in self defense, this being the import of his whole harangue. Sentence was then passed to the effect that on the following day he be hanged between the hours of two and four o'clock p.m. by the neck until dead.

At one o'clock the following day we repaired to the place of execution, where a suitable and substantial gallows had been erected. We found a large crowd of the curious already collected, some standing on and around the platform, examining the mechanism of the trap, while others were seated along the side hills engaged in talking, jesting, etc. About one-third of the motley group was women, who had come out in holiday dress to see a human being pass from life to death. Before proceeding to the gallows, we had seen the prisoner at the Hemingway, now the Platte House, where he had been taken to get his last dinner—and he did ample justice to everything set before him and was calm, cool and careless in his bearing as any of the bystanders, manifesting no concern whatever at his speedily approaching doom. The gallows had been erected on the flat midway between a line of bluffs and Cherry Creek, the former affording an excellent stand to witness the spectacle. At two o'clock the sheriff approached, bringing the halter, which he secured to the beam; after adjusting the trap, he retired and in half an hour's time was again seen approaching with the prisoner and followed by the mounted "Vigilance Committee," each carrying a drawn sword. On reaching the gallows, the prisoner, sheriff, clergyman, and two others ascended to the platform, while the Vigilance Committee formed a circle around it. After the reading of a chapter (from the bible) and a prayer by the minister, in which the victim joined, his confession was read; and then his arms were pinioned, his legs tied together, and he was shoved upon the drop without the least sign of fear or trembling; the cap was then drawn over his face, the trap was sprung, the drop fell and he hung a corpse, without a spasm, without a quiver to mark the transition from life to death. After hanging fifteen minutes, he was cut down, placed in a coffin, and delivered to his friends.

The proceeding throughout was characterized by the most perfect order and decorum and reflected much credit on those charged with the performance of this tragic duty.

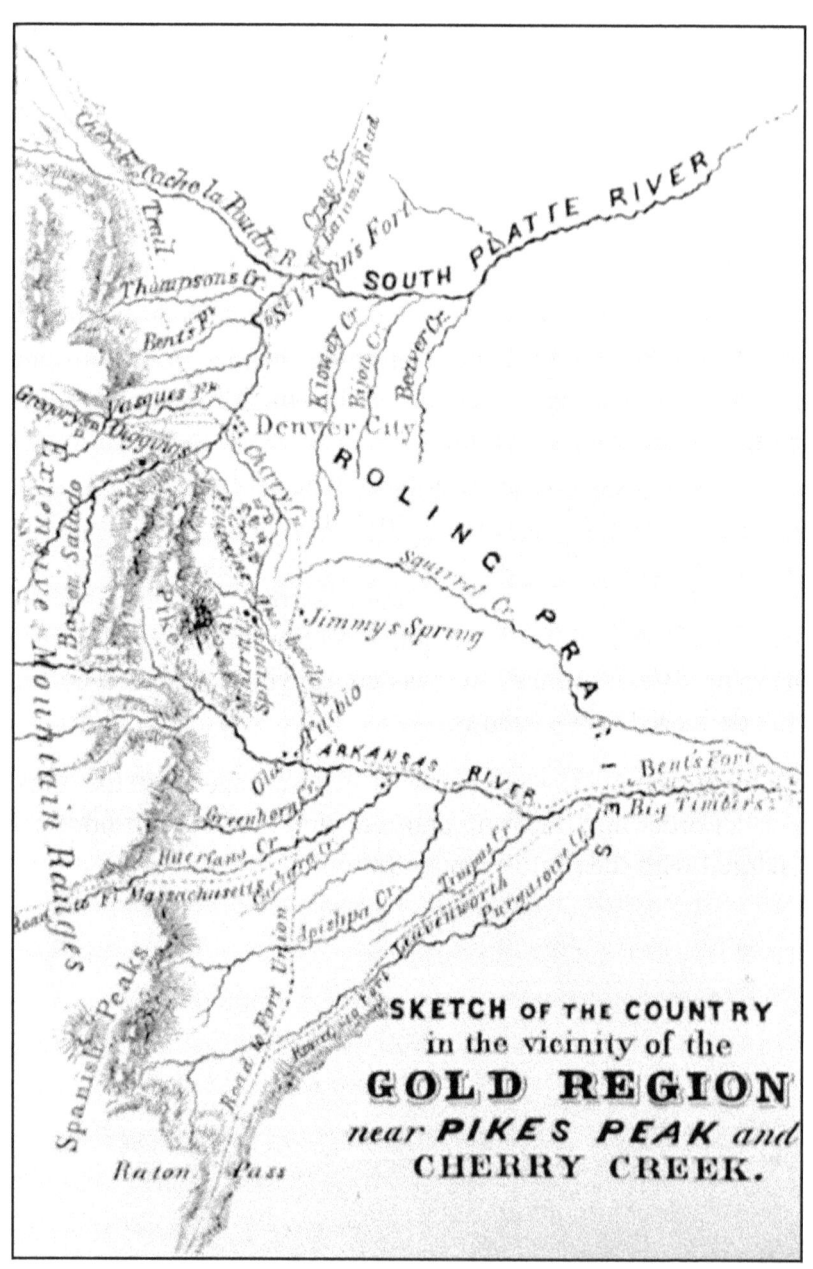

A rather accurate map from one of the many 1859-1860 guide books shows most of the main tributaries leading to the gold fields in the mountains.
Marcy, The Prarie Traveler.

LETTER X

START FOR THE MOUNTAINS—THE ROAD THERE—GOLDEN CITY—TABLE MOUNTAIN—MAKE AN ACQUAINTANCE, AND HUNT PRAIRIE DOGS—PROSPECT FOR GOLD ON CLEAR CREEK—THE ROADS LEADING UP THE MOUNTAINS—START INTO THE MOUNTAINS—THE MOUNTAINS AND SCENERY—BERGEN'S RANCHE—THE PLANTS AND FLOWERS.

After remaining a few days in Denver, we started for the mountains, glad to leave that city and its vices; we turned down upon the bottom, crossed the river (which is bridged) and after traversing the rolling plain for a distance of fifteen miles reached Golden City. This place is located in a small valley on either side of Clear Creek and bounded on the west by the first range of mountains, on the east by two large buttes known as the Table Mountains, and on the north and south by the foothills. It is very prettily located and has a population of from three to four hundred. The buildings are principally frame, well constructed and many of them painted; but previous to July 12, 1859, there was not a building erected, the only habitations being a few scattered tents. There are now several public houses, stores, groceries, and commission houses, and all doing a fair business. It has a good class of citizens and is decidedly a moral as well as model town, no gambling being permitted; and, besides, it is generally exempt from the many other vices that attach themselves to a settlement in a mining region. Clear Creek, running through its center, is a fine, large stream with a swift current, whose waters roll and foam over the rocky bed with a loud, angry murmur that can be heard some distance. The water is cold but exceedingly turbid, as it receives all the "washings" from the Gregory district, besides those carried on along its own banks and bars. It would furnish an excellent water-power, which at no late day will be taken advantage of, and it is also said to contain fine trout.

The two buttes or Table Mountains that rise up on either side of Clear Creek, or Vasquez Fork, have an irregular circumference of some five or eight miles, and rise to an altitude of more than 6,000 feet above the level of the sea, and about 1,000 above the city; they have a precipice averaging from fifty to two hundred feet along their western outline, consisting of columnar basalt, and the one known as Table Rock has a perfectly flat summit surface with a circumference, I should judge, of about ninety feet.

The mountain below this rock has a gradual slope and is covered with verdure and with fragments of the rock above, which have fallen or been hurled down by tourists that have visited it. The summit of the mountain is also flat and bears many evidences of its volcanic character, being covered in many places with volcanic rock, cellular lava, etc.; aside from the barren spaces it is covered with a rank verdure, several species of cactus, and an abundant floral vegetation; and we often saw elk and antelope grazing over its broad extent of surface. It is said that gold has been prospected there, but nothing more than its "color" has ever been raised.

The country surrounding, especially in the valleys, is very productive where irrigation is employed, and as fine vegetables are raised here as in any portion of the States. Agriculture, however, can never flourish in that region to any extent because of the shortness of the seasons.

Letter X

While encamped at Golden City we made the acquaintance of an old Missourian, who had lately arrived, bringing his family, consisting of a wife and three sons. He "allowed that if thar was gold in yon mountain, he should stop and work it out, and he had an idea that thar was a mighty smart chance for it; but if thar was not, he should get to go over to Oregon and 'squat.'" He had been an old miner in lead in Missouri, where he had always lived. He was a great hunter and in his day had brought down many a "bar" with his rifle, but he couldn't brag on his shootin' now as much as he used to when he could hit the center every time, for his "narves" were getting "onsteady" and his sight "mighty poor," yet he "allowed" if I wanted to go out and hunt prairie dogs that he would show me how that "ar" old rifle of his worked.

There were several villages of these marmots situated along the foot of the mountains, and we started out among them, but as we approached, the sharp, warning cry of the sentinels, placed here and there and seated on the summit of their houses, created a panic among the inhabitants, and each starting for their home at a full lope; on reaching which, they stopped, considering themselves safe, and arose on their haunches to look after the cause of the commotion; and taking advantage of their position and quiet, my companion and self, shot two but did not secure them, as they invariably fall into the hole; the evidence that they were shot appearing in the blood stains and fragments of meat scattered around the entrance. At the report of the guns, every dog disappeared, and the town was silent and deserted.

Passing on, we soon saw a flock of young owls seated around the entrance to a mound, and hastily running up, we secured one, who was slower in retreating than the others, but not until it was knocked senseless with a ramrod. After recovering from the shock, it began to show fight, continually hissing like a serpent and snapping at everything held toward him. My friend did not like "that ar" hiss, and "allowing" that the darned thing was "pizen," wouldn't touch it, but I persuaded him to hold my handkerchief while I lifted the creature into it, and we carried it along. Before going back, we visited a ledge of lime stone rock that was as white as snow, and decidedly the purest article I ever saw, and a kiln was being erected for the burning of it. We also visited some singular formation of white sandstone that stood out boldly from the spur of the mountain, of all shapes and forms, and here we found that the chisel of the artisan had been at work cutting out and dressing portions for building purposes. On the surrounding swells and hills, we found many ferrous and other stones of all sizes and shapes, some of which were very handsome.

When returning, the "old gentlemen," who had heard of the projected railroad through to California, wanted to know if I thought it would ever be built and said he had his doubts about it yet didn't know much about such things, never having seen one. I told him that the supposition was that the Pacific Railroad would at some day be carried through, and that the plan was feasible for the road could be carried over the mountains with a grade not to exceed fifty feet to the mile. He hoped that it might be constructed in his day; and if it was, he would be the first to pass over it.

The following day, with pan, shovel and pick, we started out to prospect for gold, following up the banks of Clear Creek to the mouth of the canyon, where we dug a small trench, sinking down through a rich surface bed of humus, then a strata of sand, finally reaching at a depth of two feet, a bed of gravel, small boulders, or round stone. This we gathered into the pan and washed, finding a large quantity of black sand, and ultimately, a small amount of "color." Gold can be found everywhere throughout the valley of this creek, in greater or lesser quantities, and the people of the town, while digging their wells, find a good prospect at the depth of twenty feet; and in so digging, they found many large fragments of rock that had been worn smooth and round by the action of water, and it is surmised that if the original channel of the creek could be discovered that they should find gold in plenty.

We carried on our operations in various localities until we obtained a very pretty and large sample of scale, or spangle gold; then we returned to our encampment with the settled conviction that a good sluice in that locality would pay, and it was determined to go the following day and stake out several claims; but our purpose had been anticipated, for we found to our disappointment that another company had taken up our coveted ground. Meanwhile, our *compagnons du voyage,* the Messrs. H. E. Rounds & Co., and to whom we felt much indebted, not only for their agreeable society, but for many favors shown us during the trip, had departed for Mountain City, and we resolved to follow. We first instituted inquiries as to which was the best road; but public opinion was as much divided on this point, as in many other relative of the country, and we were none the wiser for our efforts. Some would recommend this, that and the other; while others would tell us that there was no difference, they were all bad enough.

The roads leading up and through the mountains are four in number, including the one leading over the Jackson Hill, but which, by the by, is seldom traveled. I remember passing over it once with a yoke of cattle attached to an empty wagon and had it not been an exceedingly light one, I should have failed; for it is high and very steep, and the road for the first 200 feet leads straight up without any curve whatever; I thought, while panting with the exertion of climbing, shouting, whipping, and withal, with the carrying of a big stone with which to block the wheels, that it was decidedly the tallest traveling that I had ever done or should wish to do again. The cattle would tire out every few minutes, when both rear wheels had to be blocked, and quickly too, or I lost ground, and then it was often necessary to chain or stand upon the wheels to prevent them from rolling over the blocking. After about an hour's laborious struggle on the part of the cattle and me, we reached the summit, where we encountered a heavy shower of rain, but locking the wheels, I jumped under cover and slid down the Colorado wagon road and at nine o'clock p.m. reached Bergen's Ranche, my destination.

The other roads are known as the Old Road, the St. Vrain, Golden City, Colorado Road, and the Mount Vernon Road.

The Old Road leads from Golden City up to Golden Gate, which is located at the mouth of a canon, where there are a few buildings. This road has been well worked, yet it possesses many steep parts and pitches that are not at all comfortable to the traveler or his team. From Golden Gate the road circles around the base of the mountains with a variable grade, until we reach the level of the first range; it then follows over hills and through valleys, until we finally descend into the Gregory Mining District.

The St. Vrain, Golden City and Colorado wagon road follows the canon just south of the town. It is comparatively new and presents about the same features as the old road, being cut and carried around the sides of the mountains with a moderate grade, with now and then a steep grade that is difficult to climb. It finally traverses meadows, crosses streams, ascends mountains, leading us into the South Park, over the snowy ranges, to the Blue and Arkansas Diggings and, ultimately, to the Rio Colorado.

The Mount Vernon Road is the most southerly, and, in my judgment, the best of the mountain roads. It follows up a canyon, at the mouth of which is located the small town of

Letter X

Mount Vernon, the residence of Governor Steele. The ascent up this canyon is very gradual, and the road beyond is generally good with the exception of the "big hill," where the grade approximates closely to the perpendicular in many places; but generally, by locking the wheels and with care in driving, the descent is safely made. Reaching Clear Creek, which the road follows up and finally crosses, we passed up along the north branch into Pleasant Valley, Lake Gulch, to Missouri City and the mining districts. These various roads, with the exception of that up the Jackson Hill, are toll roads; one dollar and seventy-five cents per team being charged via the Old Road, and one dollar by the others.

Before leaving Golden City, very favorable reports from the head waters of the Arkansas reached us, and we determined to proceed over to California Gulch; and finding a friend who was about to depart for that region, we made arrangements to transfer a part of our load into his wagon, add a yoke of cattle, and accompany him. His party consisted of himself and wife, together with five men, whom he was to board through for fifteen dollars per head; and with our party of three made up a company of ten, and we had a freight of about 2,500 pounds with a team of three yoke of cattle to draw it. On the afternoon of the following day we started on our trip, proceeding via the St. Vrain, Golden City and Colorado Road. Our progress was slow for the day was sultry, and the air was found to be so light that frequent halts were necessary in order to rest and "blow." While proceeding up the canyon, several of the company started on in advance of the team, to keep the track clear and to signal us if there were any wagons coming down, for the road is too narrow to permit the passage of teams, except at the turn-outs provided every half mile or so. We traveled on quite comfortably for the distance of two miles, when we reached a steeper and stonier grade, down which was trickling the waters of a spring, making the track muddy and exceedingly slippery.

On attempting the rise of this, the team was stalled, and our hopes of reaching the summit that night looked dubious. Trial after trial was made, but the rear wheels were "snub up" against a ledge of rock. The cattle at each pull would slip, often falling on their knees, and the leaders finally commenced baulking, and we began to calculate on the chances of remaining in status quo over night. But one more trial was decided upon, and the "boarders" were called back to assist. The cattle were then changed; a man was stationed to lift at each wheel, and one to superintend the blocking, while the others, armed with whips and sticks, stood by the cattle, one or two on the off side to prevent the cattle from turning off the embankment into the deep ravine below. "Now boys, are ye all ready?" "Aye! aye!" was responded. "Then heave her up!" And the thwack, thwack, of the heavy gads, the hoarse yells of the drivers, and the cry of "she moves!" and "keep her moving!" of the men at the wheels made up a din, which aside from the reverberated echoes of the mountains, would have put life into duller bullocks than ours. The result of our combined efforts was a move of six feet, which was encouraging, and we repeated the process and soon reached the next level, where, as night was fast approaching, we concluded to stop until morning, and the cattle were unyoked and turned up the mountain to feed; then to pacify the boarders and keep our spirits up, a bottle of ginger brandy and a box of cigars were circulated.

Near by was a bough-covered log shanty, which had once been occupied by the laborers on the road, and which had been erected over an excavation made in the side of the mountain. Into this the majority went, built up a fire for the night air was cold and frosty, and seating themselves on the banks on either side, lit their cigars, and listened to an old Californian, who related his adventures among the Sierra Nevada, many of which were very apropos to the occasion. Not wishing to spend the night within the cabin, which did not smell very sweet, and besides, fearing the

Letter X

presence of those abominable crawlers which are so frequently met with in the mountains, to wit, body-lice—myself and two others went to the tent which had been erected and there spent the night.

We were astir bright and early the ensuing morning, and after a hasty breakfast of coffee and pancakes had been eaten, prepared to renew our journey, and after a mile further travel, reached the summit, where we found a good road which led through a small meadow carpeted with an abundant growth of good grass, among which was interspersed a brilliant flora. We were now at an altitude of about 2,000 feet above the level of the plain, and many of us found it exceedingly difficult to travel, owing to the lightness of the air. During the morning's travel we passed several stock ranches, where cattle are herded and kept at an expense of from one to one and a half dollars per month.

Our road occasionally led over stubborn hills thickly covered with tall pines and firs; at other times it wound through gorges and ravines; now and then traversing pleasant valleys bounded on every side by lofty mountains; and occasionally we could see the glistening snow peaks of the great axis situated some thirty miles beyond. At noon we stopped at the Texan Ranche, where a gallon of milk was bought, for which we paid sixty cents; a kettle of mush was manufactured, then we spread ourselves and dishes beneath the shadow of a towering pine, and there in an incredibly short space of time, the contents of both kettle and pail were put out of sight, filling one of the vacuums so much abhorred by nature.

Near night and after many hard pulls, we descended into a pretty valley, where Bergen's Ranche is located. Here some bread was bought, for which twenty-five cents a pound was paid, and we proceeded on for a few miles and encamped in a small dell for the night. Soon after encamping, a drizzly, cold rain set in, which put a damper on the fire, lit up the wrath of the cook, and kept us in a stew for supper; but finally a few wafer-like pancakes and a cup of tea were set before us, which were partaken of in a graceless manner. Then creeping under our blankets with an allotted space not to exceed 2 x 6, and a slim cotton shelter over us, we were soon oblivious to trouble. But an uninterrupted sleep under the circumstances was by no means certain, and it chanced that our sleep was many times disturbed, for there were eight of us stowed away here on an area of ten feet square, and the latitude for motion was rather limited. Some of the company were subject to "bad dreams" and "vocal noses" and between the discordant and wheezy piping on the one side, and the involuntary kicks and starts on the other, it was surprising that slumber did not leave us; but the relief of fatigue was too powerful to indulge in many waking fits, and it was only when receiving a well directed hit that it operated as an "eye-opener"—when we would retaliate on these sleeping pugilists, awakening them to a sense of their senseless actions.

The following day our road led through several small but beautiful parks with little rivulets coursing through them, and surrounded by an amphitheatre of massive pine-clad hills. During the day's drive the teams were several times stalled and once in a slough, the result of careless driving—three wheels being sunk to the hub in mire, and we had to discharge half the load before getting out. This occurred at the foot of a high hill, proceeding up which the cattle would not *Gee* as much as they were told, and the consequence was that the fore axle was brought in contact with a stump, and the balance of the load was discharged. We shoved the wagon around, when it proceeded up the hill, leaving the load behind to be "backed" by the company up a steep height of over two hundred feet; I had occasion to measure it several times, as well as the

Letter X

others, and in no very pleasant mood either. Our party was getting tired of this method of travel and resolved to unship our portion of the load after reaching the "Junction" and start back for our wagon, fully confident that if we continued on in this manner that not only ourselves, but our cattle, would be "used up" before reaching our destination, for the road was becoming more and more rough as we neared the dividing ridge between the eastern and western slope.

On reaching the Junction, our plan was made known, much to the satisfaction of the others concerned. Our goods were then taken out, and the next morning our friend and his boarders went on, and we remained behind. During the day we found a teamster returning from Tarryall, who took us back to Bergen's Ranche, where we remained until our wagon was brought up from Golden City.

Bergen's Ranche is one of the best within the mountains, not only for the herding of cattle and the storing of goods, but in the affording of entertainment to the traveler. It is very pleasantly situated in a valley, which is partly covered with tall pines, and that portion devoted to pasture has an abundance of grass.

In speaking of the mountains and their scenery, it is impossible to convey any correct idea either of one or the other. The mountains, seen from a distance, present a vast series of ridges and cones, that rise higher and higher, until the wearied eye rests on those covered with perpetual snow. The highest peak seen is that known as Long's, which rises to an altitude of some 18,000 feet (actually 14,255 feet) above the level of the Gulf of Mexico. It is surrounded by large mountains and is situated back in the Cache le Poudre River country, which stream courses around its base. While viewing these ponderous masses of earth and rock that have been thrown up here, mid-way between the waters of the Atlantic and Pacific, the idea suggested to my mind was that they served the purpose of a mighty balance between the two—maintaining equilibrium between the two great oceans. A nearer view of them discloses features that are fully as instructive as interesting. In threading their devious channels and looking through the dells and valleys, one no longer wonders where the peculiar soil of the plains comes from, for here on all sides we witness the debris of degradation and decay that is continually being carried forward in the large blocks and masses of disintegrated rock that have fallen from their sides and summits. Every variety of rock is seen cropping out, with various inclinations and dips, from the primitive granite at their apex, and the transition strata surrounding, to the various secondary formations seen everywhere; and though in foreign climes, nature may have more bountifully diversified the sublime, yet, nowhere has she more liberally bestowed her grandeur and beauty than amid the Rocky Mountains.

Many of the mountains are covered with a thick growth of timber, among which may be mentioned a variety of Pines, with their dark green foliage, and long pendulous cones; and the traveler, pursuing his way through them, is often invigorated by the spicy aroma which they exhale. Among those seen in various localities, I may mention the *Pinus Banksiana, Pinus Variabilis* (Spruce Pine) and *Palustris.* The *Populus Tremuloides* (Quaking Asp) is also common, besides several varieties of the *Abies,* such as the *Abies Canadensis, Abies Balsamea* (Balsam Spruce), and *Pendulata,* together with the *Thugo Occidentalis* (Arbor Vitae) and *Juniperus Communis;* and we notice a variety of mosses, some of which are extremely handsome, and one in particular was noticed, just creeping from without the snow and bearing a very delicate tri-colored flower—the red, white and blue. The three great parks, or meadows, situated within the mountains are a pleasing and remarkable feature, being the paradise of this broken region, carpeted with a heavy verdure, and a multitudinous flora, where a botanist might spend the year around, and they are surrounded by an amphitheater of mountains and gorgeous scenery.

The evidence of volcanic action throughout the mountains is everywhere present; we see it in their shape and formation and in the fragments of trap rock, scoriaceous stones, cellular lava and pumice scattered here and there in profusion; and besides this, we are often called to notice the various wrecks of the diluvian period, seeing here and there large masses of rock unconnected with any adjacent geological formations, and we see it too in the mighty "washes" and the new formations from "slides" that occurred when the waters washed and rolled in mighty columns from the west, deluging the world.

The mountain streams, fed from the melting snows, are numerous; the larger of which roll and roar through the ravines and canons at an impetuous speed; while the smaller ones glide smoothly over their pebbly bed, meandering through the valleys and dells until they join their more boisterous neighbors; their banks being skirted with willows, bushes and vines, and some of Flora's brightest creations, and their water as bright and clear as crystal and as cold as ice, often containing fine trout.

The plants and flowers that thrive and bloom on the mountain sides and in the valleys and meadows are various and beautiful; but I shall attempt no description of them, and it would be vain for the poet or painter to attempt it, for they could not do them justice. While we were traveling over the mountains, I gathered as many specimens as I could, forming a *hortus siccus* (dry garden). The soil of the mountains seems to be of great floral fertility; but I have often wondered at seeing them blooming beneath the shadow of the snow and grow so luxuriantly in the fissures and crevices of rocks and in the gloomy canyons (pronounced *kanyons).* Those found rank principally among the orders of the *Compositae, Companulaceae, Labiatae,*

Coniferae and *Leguminosae.* Among the varieties of these, I mention the *Chrysanthemum Vulgare, Septopoda Brachypoda,* and several species of the *Coreopsis,* the *C. Verticillata, C. Tinctoria,* together with the *Bidens Frondoso (*Burr Marigold). We also find along the damp rocks and streams, the *Campanula Rotundifolia* (Rock Bell Flower), and several other varieties of *Campanula.* The *Monardo Fistulosa* (Bergamot) is common, together with several species of *Scutillaria, Phlox, Covolvulus, Asclepia, Lilium, Amorpha,* and we frequently see a very pretty white flowing vine, the *Clematis Lasiantha,* and several varieties of the *Delphinium* (Larkspur), Geranium, *Viola,* and the wild Columbine (*Aquilegia Canadensis).* The class of *Rosa* is well represented and pleasantly perfumed, as are most of the flowers.

There are several varieties of Cactus found on the summits and sides of the mountains, growing amid the rocks, bearing white and scarlet colored flowers. Besides the *Opuntia Vulgaris,* so common upon the plains, bearing a large, brilliant yellow flower, we find the *Cereus Truncatus, Cereus Flagelliformis* (Snake Cactus), *Superbus,* and a species of the Melon Cactus.

Among the berries found is the *Amelanchier Canadensis* (Service Berry), *Pyrus Arbutifolia* (Choke Berry), *Ribes Strigosus* and *Occidentalis* (Raspberries), and the Mulberry *(Ribes Chamaemorus).* The Currants seen are the *Ribes Rubrum* and *Ribes Aureum,* known as the Lewis & Clark's Currant. The Gooseberries are the *Ribes Rotundifolium* and *Ribes Cynosbati,* and we find the *Cerasus Virginiana* (Choke Cherries) growing on the sides of the buttes, and the *Prunus Americana* (Yellow Plum), and the *Vitus Cordifolia* (Frost Grape) are often found along the borders of the streams. The *Allium Triflorum* (Leek) is found on the mountain sides; we often gathered them for use, and they afforded quite a relish. The wild Potato (*Psorolea Esculenta),* wild Oats, wild Barley, etc., were also frequently noticed, together with several varieties of Flax, among which was the *Linum Perenne* (Perennial Flax).

I have thus, but imperfectly, noted some of the botanical productions of the mountains, and which but poorly serves to convey any ideas of the diversity that exists there; but there are those who are directing their attention to this subject, and who will be better able to speak of the botany of that region.

LETTER XI

START FOR THE CLEAR CREEK DIGGINGS—OUR OPERATIONS THERE AND THE OPERATIONS OF OTHERS—HOW MINERS LIVE AND WORK, AND WHY THEY ARE NOT SUCCESSFUL—MOUNTAIN GAME—SNOWY RANGE—UTE INDIANS—PROSPECTING—GREGORY'S DIGGINGS—MOUNTAIN CITY, MISSOURI CITY, AND CENTRAL CITY—SPRING GULCH, NEVADA GULCH, LAKE GULCH, ETC.—QUARTZ MILLS AND QUARTZ MINING—SPECULATION—QUARTZ HILL—SALTING CLAIMS, ETC.

During our stay at Bergen's Ranche, the news that we received from the Arkansas and Blue River Diggings rather served to cool our ardor for proceeding to that region; the many returning "gold seekers" telling us that it was impossible to secure a claim in "California Gulch," as they had all been taken, and hundreds were there idle and about to return. The same was also said of the paying gulches at Tarryall on the Blue River; yet there was a large tract of country there remaining unexplored, allowing plenty of room for prospecting; but we, like many others, disliked spending the short season in discovering and looking after uncertainties, which feeling was very natural, and one perhaps too general. Men had rather go where gold had been and was still being found and risk the chances of obtaining a claim, than go abroad seeking uncertainty, though there might be a hundred localities of hidden treasure that only awaited development. This is the reason why we find so many centered in particular localities—for instance, the Gregory and Russel districts, where hundreds were seen idling away their time (there being no vacant claims) and complaining of the greediness of their more fortunate predecessors. It also explains the slow development of the vast mineral wealth of that region, as well as furnishing the clue to the constant stampede back to the States.

Under the existing circumstances, it was decided to defer our trip to the Arkansas River mines, and we prepared to proceed over to Clear Creek and follow up its banks and bars, which was reported as second to none in the mountains for its yield of gold. As we did not wish the trouble of a wagon, the roads being new and unfinished, we tried the experiment of packing our mining tools, provisions and bedding upon the cattle, and for that purpose sewed several stout bags together for saddle pouches. Then loading upon one ox our provisions and mining tools and transferring to the other our bedding, tents and rubber clothing, we started, one leading each ox, while the other carried the gun and tent poles. Our road led through a succession of pretty valleys covered with a variety of grasses and flowers and bordered by smooth grassy hills. While we were traveling, the swaying motion of the cattle so disturbed the position of their packs that frequent halts were necessary in order to make adjustments. To correct their tendency to slip forward, we added a breeching made from a strip of canvass; but we had not proceeded far before one of the bullocks, considering this affix as interfering with his freedom of motion, began to evince a rebellious spirit and commenced a series of jumps and kicks that were ludicrous in the extreme and resulted in a scattering of the miscellaneous contents of the saddle bags. Shovels, picks and pans, cooking utensils, knives, forks and spoons, bags of rice, coffee and sugar, together with a batch of biscuit, and diverse other articles were sent flying in all directions. The freak so convulsed us with laughter that we were powerless in preventing anything more than the escape of the animal, who having disburdened himself of his pack, breeching and all, stood calmly surveying the mischief he had created.

As soon as possible, we set to work gathering up the fragments. Securing the pack more firmly than before, but leaving off the offensive posterior arrangement that had been the occasion of such a furious "back action" on his part and such merriment on ours. Upon resuming our journey we soon reached Spring Valley Ranche, just above which the road descends, winding down a high mountain to Clear Creek. Here we had more trouble with the packs, for in descending the many steep pitches they would slip over upon the neck and horns of the animals, occasioning many delays for their readjustment. Before reaching our destination, we were abundantly satisfied that loading cattle with such paraphernalia might answer as a *dernier resort* (last resort), and only when unable to shoulder it ourselves. We reached Union District at sunset and pitched our tent on a high level bank of the creek near the abode of a party of miners in as wild and rugged a region as can be found within the mountains; high mountains rising up on every side with abrupt and jagged outlines, their sides strewed with immense blocks of materials transported from distant summits, while here and there in the rifts and cracks stood an isolated pine or juniper. In the chasm below rolled the boiling waters of the creek, leaping and roaring on its way to the Platte; its banks on either side and the bars below showing where the miners were at work by the ditches and sluices, the excavations, the piles of earth and boulders that had been thrown out in every direction.

We soon made the acquaintance of the miners here, one company of whom (consisting of four) had been operating here

Letter XI

about a week but without much success; and three of them were now considering the propriety of returning back to the States, being frank to confess that their united labors here had yielded them but about three dollars, "which wouldn't pay," and as their provisions were about exhausted, there was seemingly no other alternative. The other of the party was for remaining yet longer, confident that the claim would eventually pay if it was properly worked; but his companions were dispirited and thought differently and expressed it as their opinion that the country was a d__d humbug, and the sooner they started for home the better.

We bought their sluice boxes, and they assigned to us all their right and title to four claims, which were located one-half mile up the creek and two miles below Grass Valley Bar. The ensuing morning, we were put in possession of the property and commenced to prospect it; we first filled our pan with dirt taken from the bank that our friends had been "sluicing" from and obtained merely a "color;" but in another division of the claim we got from three to ten cents to the pan, which we considered good enough and commenced locating our sluice boxes. As the water of the creek was low, we had to sink the ditch or race deeper and throw out a wing-dam into the stream before we could get a sufficient fall of water for our purpose. This occupied the better part of two days

Gold panning was the preferred method of looking for signs of gold in the new "diggings, although the prospectors soon learned to look for a nearby vein. Thayer.

and was decidedly laborious work, especially the carrying of heavy boulders fifteen and twenty feet into the stream, where the current was so strong that it would carry the smaller stones downstream and even disturb those weighing fifty pounds and upwards. The creek at this point had a width of thirty feet, and its waters rushed with a mad fury by us, and to have been fallen into it would have been death, as it had innumerable rocks.

Adjoining us were a company of four from Missouri, who intimated that they were doing well, "making grub," etc., but on becoming better acquainted by a frequent interchange of visits, we learned that as yet their claim had not paid above thirty cents per day to the man, but they were still digging and hoping that when they reached the "bed rock" something better would turn up.

Across the creek, nearly opposite our claims, were a company of seven persons who were mining with a like success; but the next claim above theirs was paying five dollars per day to the man; it was being worked by an old California miner.

We were ready to commence operations on our claim the fourth of July, 1860, and started after an early breakfast to work out our patriotism with shovel and pick in the "diggings." We had two inches of water in the ditch, and removing the dam we soon had it coursing through our sluice, which consisted of four boxes or troughs, each sixteen feet long, so constructed that they could be joined together, one end slipping within that of another—the second and third containing a riffle frame of twelve bars each. The bank or bar in which we were digging arose twelve feet above the river and extended back for a distance of fifty feet to the base of the mountain, and there was stripping of from three to four feet before reaching the pay dirt, which consisted of a brown ochre-colored earth and fine gravel, and which was obtained by pecking around the

Letter XI

boulders. These boulders of various sizes, colors and forms differed in composition; some of them would weigh a ton and upward, and the form was generally oval, worn perfectly smooth by water. This whole bar, as well as the many others met with, was composed of these boulders, cemented together with earth in the proportion of three-fourths of the former to one-fourth of the latter.

In working, it was necessary that one should constantly peck in order to furnish dirt to be sluiced, which another shoveled into the sluice at the head of the first box, and then the small stones would roll and lodge between the riffle bars, requiring the presence of a third person to keep them clear and throw out the larger stones. We thus worked for a period of six hours, each speculating on the result when the water was turned off and we turned our attention to cleaning up. The first riffle frame was taken out, and the contents put into the pan; and we proceeded with it to the still water, to wash it, while the others cleaned up the contents of the second frame and looked for stray scales along the sides and seams of the boxes. The operation of "panning" requires much skill for its proper performance; there is a peculiar motion to be given to the pan, which only experience can confer, and much care is necessary in separating and turning off the black sand, which has a specific gravity almost equal to gold. This black sand is always present in large quantities and is magnetic, but its presence is no sure indication of gold—not so much as the small pellets of clay stone iron that are found. The result of our day's work was finally known—the first riffle yielded about forty cents and the second not to exceed ten, making in all fifty cents for six hours' hard labor, a poor return for the muscle expended.

The gold found in the bars occurs in the form of scales or spangles of all sizes and shapes, and it is sometimes found in *pepitas* (seeds) averaging from the size of a pin's head to that of a pea, and occasionally nuggets are found, but these latter are rare. I have, however, seen them weighing from twelve to fifty dollars. That taken from the shoals of the creeks is much finer, called "dust," although it occurs at times in crystals, assuming a *brancy* (dendritic) form and also in small thin *luminae*, called "float-gold." I shall have occasion to speak of this later further on.

The gold found in the bars, plateaus, and shoals, does not present the appearance of having been thrown up and scattered in all directions by volcanic action, but rather as though its mother quartz had suffered disintegration, crumbled to dust, leaving the metal as it was made, in all conceivable shapes and sizes. And then again, by the constant attrition of water that formed these bars, they have been cut up into grains and particles according to the degree of attrition to which they have been exposed—thus in the shoals, having been subjected in the greatest degree, is consequently found the finest. That found in the "placers" or "dry diggings" is often found with quartz adhering to it—of which I saw several fine specimens—and this, not having been subjected to the friction of a strong current of water, retains its original configuration.

We continued on working our claim with about the same result as previously mentioned. We had reached the "bedrock," which seemed to have a favorable dip, or inclination, but yet the "cleaning up" each day showed no increase in the deposit of the precious metal within the riffle frame. There was a fault somewhere, and it was either in the locality, the sluice, the riffles, or us. That it was in the location, we could not be positive, for the prospect that we got with the pan inclined me to the belief that the locality was good, yet I by no means indulged the opinion of many that gold could be found anywhere and everywhere, for it is found only in particular localities and attended by peculiar indications and circumstances. That it was in the

Letter XI

sluice, riffles, etc., was more evident. The sluice had been constructed of rough boards, poorly joined, and the riffles were rough and uneven, and the spaces between the bars were too wide. And, besides, they were not properly formed or adapted so the flow of water through the sluice was not properly regulated, generally carrying too much and consequently forcing many particles of gold over and under the imperfect riffles, and not having an amalgamating box affixed to the tail of the sluice, much of the gold was lost.

Some of the party were getting discouraged and ill at ease, confident that the location was bad, and thought that we had better go over to Gregory's; and our neighbors, who were as unsuccessful as ourselves, and for the same reasons often came over to sympathize with us and to receive sympathy, and the matter was talked over. We had been living in our tent, which had been spread upon the bar above the works in the midst of several tall pines; but the location, though as good as the district afforded, was not desirable, the surface being sloping and uneven, and the abode of innumerable ants and bugs that had seemingly made our tent their headquarters. Not a night passed that we were not more or

There was always a race to every new report of gold, but all the good spots were usually gone before word even leaked out.
Ingersoll, *Knocking Around the Rockies.*

less disturbed by their rambles over our person, they now and then giving us a hungry nip. Our life here was decidedly a rough one. The nights were cold and chilly, and it was utterly impossible to keep warm; and we would get up at day break, almost benumbed, build a fire, thaw out, and prepare our breakfast, then proceed to work, which was continued until eleven o'clock, when we would prepare dinner and lounge around until two o'clock and proceed again to work on developing our muscles and claim. At four o'clock we "cleaned up," and as soon as the result was known, we returned to the tent in no pleasant mood, dissatisfied, disheartened, and the majority about ready to clear out.

A miner's life is a hard and laborious one; cut off from all the refinements and comforts of life; living in a tent or rude shanty; making up their bed at night with a blanket or two on the ground or on a frame of poles; cooking their meals over a fire in the open air and eating them on a log; and surrounded by dirt and filth that is constantly accumulating, and which, in some localities that I have seen, is breeding disease and propagating vermin. The "bill of fare" of the miner is not very extensive, especially when he is removed from market and dependent on the stores he brought with him. It generally consists of pancakes made from flour and water with the addition of a little soda and cream of tartar, a strip or two of fried bacon, and a cup of tea or coffee. Sometimes soda bread or a corn cake is made, and some dried apples stewed. This is their meal for day after day, and notwithstanding its sameness, some seem to relish and grow fat upon it, always making up in quantity what is lacking in quality. Many amid the mountains have good appetites, and it is surprising to see how much food they consume at a meal. I have seen a company of four men sit down and eat a large loaf of bread, eight slices of bacon, and a four quart basin of apple sauce, besides drinking a quart of coffee each, and then they were hardly satisfied.

Letter XI

Work in the diggings is a toilsome and monotonous occupation; and the extremes of weather, hard work and poor food often makes the life of the miner almost intolerable; frequently toiling beneath a broiling sun and in the chilly water for weeks and weeks, the monotony of the time and scene seldom relieved, and his labor generally poorly recompensed.

The greatest difficulty that the miner has to contend with in the bar diggings is the many large boulders met with, and which have to be rolled aside; at times they are so large that much time and labor is expended in their removal. Aside from this, the work is comparatively easy. In the gulches, men are more exposed to the sun and are obliged to work in water more or less, and it is not unusual to see them at work, standing in mud and water to their knees while feeding the sluices; persons at work in these gulches, from their constant exposures to heat and cold, soon lose a portion of their constitutional stability—suffering often from sickness.

Our mining operations on Clear Creek were finally terminated, together with those of our friends, whose verdict was that their claims would not pay to work, and we knew that ours had not, and the majority were for proceeding over to the Gregory's district; while the remainder who had a sufficient experience in mining, intended starting home. Our success here had been like that of thousands of others, who had left their homes with big expectations and greedy eyes, intending to make a fortune in less than no time, without even counting the cost or thinking of disappointment; and it only required a few days' hard work with the shovel and pick to dissipate their wild speculations and send them back to cry "humbug."

Many had started from their farms, their shops and stores with no knowledge of mining; and on reaching the mountains, not finding gold scattered over the surface or in every locality they chanced to sink their shovels, were disconcerted. They knew nothing of the circumstances under which gold is found or of indications that pointed to its discovery; and, perchance, they stumbled upon a good prospect, they were but little acquainted with the proper method of working it to advantage. Obtaining some rough boards from the mill, they nailed them together, forming their sluice, and then, with no tools but a hatchet and jack-knife, would whittle out their riffle frame and bars. I have seen them so poorly constructed that when set within the sluice, not one in its whole length set snugly down, and I would see the black sand streaming out from their under surface. Is it strange that such miners were not successful?

And there were those who had not come with the requisites for working—these were a tough, hardy constitution and capital. The first of these were indispensible, for no man can win a fortune from the mountains without health; and in mining, a man's powers of endurance are fully tested for the labor required is severe and weakening. And then the other requisite, money, is as much a *sine qua non* (without which not) there, as it is in the States, for the successful prosecution of business. But the thousands who went to the gold fields seemingly took no thought of this and consequently suffered disappointment.

There are also many other reasons why men are not successful in their operations in that country. Some have not sufficient stability of character, and besides they are so greedy that every new discovery that reaches their ears makes them dissatisfied with their own claims, and they pack up and start somewhere else, leaving a certainty for an uncertainty; and there are others who are decidedly too lazy to succeed there, or anywhere.

Again there is undoubtedly a question about the country being so pregnant with gold, as represented by those sanguine individuals that are interested. That gold exists in abundance in

Letter XI

some particular localities is certain, and that rich deposits may exist elsewhere is a reasonable conjecture; but that it is strewn indiscriminately over the whole surface is untrue. The gold deposits in the Rocky Mountains have not, as yet, been fully developed, nor will they be for years. The mountains, in my opinion, are rich in minerals, not only in gold, but silver, copper, and iron; and I have seen some specimens of platinum that had been found near the head waters of the Arkansas.

Rocky Mountain sheep were definitely agile and sure-footed, but not to the extent that is shown in this drawing. *Harper's Weekly.*

Extensive beds of coal are also found, some specimens of which I have seen, breaking with a bright shining fracture, and containing an excess of bituminous and volatile matter, being very combustible. Veins of pure alum are also found in some localities.

Before leaving for the Gregory district, we spent several days in prospecting and hunting. There is a variety of game seen in some portions, especially in the vicinity of the snowy range, which lies some thirty-five miles back from Golden City. The mountains constituting this range look dreary and barren, there being very little vegetation seen on their sides, consisting principally of rocks that crop out in all directions. In some places we see massive walls of slate and granite rising up, piercing the snow that caps their summits.

Among the game met with and found within the mountains is the mountain sheep (*argali ovis montanoe*), which are seen in small flocks on the mountains. Their color is a grayish fawn with a yellow line down the back, and their appearance approximates closely that of the goat that inhabits the mountains. Their body is full and round with long slender legs, and the horns of the male are very thick, large and heavy, advancing in front of the eyes, assuming the spiral form. It is said that when jumping down a precipitous height, they turn a somersault, striking upon the base of the horns. Antelopes are also seen, together with elk, and *cervus macrourus* (long tailed deer, short tailed deer, jumping deer, etc.), as it is variously called. The class of marmots are also common, from the mouse to the bear, of which last there are several species—the black bear, cinnamon bear as it is termed, and the grizzly bear (*urus ferox),* which is the largest and most formidable animal in North America. The puma is also often seen, sometimes called the Rocky Mountain lion; and strange tales often reached us of its ferocity in attacking men, but there was more fable than fact about it, I think. There are also two varieties of fox—the red fox (*canis vulvus*) and the silver gray fox, having a gray fur mingled with black. The beaver (*caster fiber*) is also common on some of the streams, and we often came across their dams. The mink and martin are also said to exist here, but this variety of animal was more frequent at the foot of the mountain and along the Platte.

The birds that we saw were magpies (*corvus pica*) or the *pica hudsonica* of Lewis and Clark. Numerous blue jays (*garrulous cristatus*) were seen flying and screaming among the trees of the mountain sides, and several species of woodpecker are also found. We frequently noticed a peculiar and beautiful species

Letter XI

of yellow bird, having black wings and a red head, fluttering among the pines.

The Indians occupying the mountains are located on the western slope and are known as the Utes. There are two tribes of them—one of which is said to be friendly, and the other hostile to the whites. Kit Carson is said to be their agent. The Arapahos make frequent sallies against these tribes but are seldom victorious in their battles; the Utes being well-supplied with fire arms, consisting of guns and revolvers, which gives them a decided advantage over the Arapahos, who are principally armed with lances, bows and arrows, etc. The Utes are the tools of the Mormons and are principally concerned in committing outrages upon the emigrants to Oregon and California, and they have at times interrupted the Pony Express, killing the riders.

In the spring of 1859, John Gregory discovered a rich gold vein on the North Fork of Clear Creek, which immediately brought hundreds of men (and women) to the spot. Richardson, *Beyond hte Mississippi.*

Prospecting has been carried on to a considerable extent in the various localities of the mountains; and in traversing through the mining country, we cannot fail to notice the many holes and trenches that have been dug in the mountain sides, the gulches, ravines, and in the bars and shoals of the streams. They vary in size, shape and depth, some of them resembling a new cut grave in appearance; and in truth, many of them are more than graves in the matter of resemblance, for the hopes and the ambition of more than one fortune seeker lie buried in their depths. During our stay in the mountains, we prospected up and down the borders of Clear Creek, Bear Creek, and through the intervening country; many times receiving a fair sample of gold but more often did not succeed in raising its color. We often found good prospects in localities on the mountain side but so far removed from water that it would not pay to work.

At last we started for Gregory's—going back to Bergen's for our wagon and from there taking a branch road that led us after a distance of about five miles to the Mount Vernon Road. We soon reached that point of it where it turns down the "big hill" and leaving our team at the approach, we started down the first declivity to notice some of its features, and they were decidedly unpleasant. We could not see the whole of the descent before us, which was three-quarters of a mile in length, yet we saw enough of it to convince us that it was not easy, and withal, a dangerous road to travel. The road was narrow and in many places, rocky, bounded on one side by a deep gulf, and made up of a series of pitches having about the slant of a gothic roof. After locking three wheels we started down, but before proceeding far, the coupling on one side gave way, and it was only with speedy and well directed efforts that we prevented our establishment from going down with a rush and being precipitated into the ravine below; but jumping on the spokes of each back wheel, while the driver ran in front of the cattle applying vigorous strokes on their noses, the catastrophe was averted.

Letter XI

We continued to ride on the wheels, now and then digging in the heels of our boots into the earth when reaching the perpendicular slants, where the cattle would often slip and slide over the wet clay surfaces that now and then were presented. Our momentum at times was alarming, and we anxiously looked forward to the termination. Finally we caught sight of the toll house below, and rounding the next point and finding a straight road, we let the machine buzz; arriving at the gate, where one dollar was demanded, which was counted out after remarking to the collector that the company ought to award premiums to those who succeeded in getting safely down. He was inclined to think that they might but told us that the road was soon to be altered, and I presume that it has since been changed.

Proceeding on along the border of Clear Creek for several miles, we crossed the stream entering the gorge through which flows the North Branch, a stream of some size, and which the road frequently crosses, sometime following up its bed some distance. Mining operations are carried on quite extensively along its bars and banks; and it was here that we first saw the operation of drifting into the side of the mountain, and which was carried on quite successfully. One company had taken out several nuggets, one of which I saw was worth sixteen dollars and fifty cents and was as fine a specimen as I ever saw. The company gave us the privilege of washing a pan of dirt from their claim, which yielded about five cents of pure scale gold, having a bright yellow color. They had drifted into the mountain, or which was more properly a slide from it, to the extent of fourteen feet and found that the claim was paying better each day.

We encamped for the night on a side hill in the locality of their claim, spreading our tent beside the road and turning our cattle up the mountain to feed. During the night a heavy storm of rain fell upon us, but the sky cleared up the next morning, and

This street scene from Gregory's Gukch shows how quickly the town built up. More logs for cabins being skidded in at he upper left.
Frank Lesilie's Illustrated Newspaper.

we continued on to Gregory's, traversing some miserable road that had been rendered muddy and slippery by the heavy rain of the preceding night, and often leading us through rocky defiles and through the bed of the stream, which I presume we crossed twenty times before proceeding a mile.

The miners throughout the gulch had suffered more or less from the heavy rain, which had inundated their mines, destroyed their pumps and disturbed their sluices; and we found many of them at work clearing up the wreck. Some, who had previously suffered much damage from the same cause, were discouraged; and we saw them gathering up their effects for a move to some other locality.

During the morning drive, we saw a rude quartz mill, worked by water power, consisting of four heavy wooden stamps, steel shod, and which mill they stated to be doing well.

Letter XI

We finally entered Pleasant Valley and proceeded through it to Lake Gulch at the head of which we encamped, having reached the far-famed Gregory District. After encamping, a violent hail storm occurred, which was one of the most severe that we had encountered during our journey across the plains or while amid the mountains. The hail that fell was very large and came so thick and fast that the ground was soon covered with icy balls that were an inch or more deep. Gregory, after whom this district is named, is one of the pioneer miners of the Rocky Mountains, and his discoveries here, together with Russel's, have built up and peopled the thriving towns we now find here.

This is one of the largest mining districts within the mountains, and the one that has and is still yielding the largest amount of gold. It is the great center of mining interests, and undoubtedly will ever remain so with the majority of the quartz mills in operation in the mountains being located here. So far, it is here that they have been most successful. The gulches throughout the district have generally paid but are now pretty well worked out, and quartz lodes are superseding them.

The gulches are lined with frame and log buildings, with many tents scattered among them. At the fork of the north branch of Clear Creek, where Spring, Nevada and Eureka Gulches all terminate in Gregory's, is located what is termed Mountain City, and where are located the Post Office, Hinckley & Co.'s Express Office, the Courthouse, Recorder's Office, etc. The continuation above this is known as Central City, where there are many stores, shops, restaurants and boarding houses. Continuing up the mountain above Spring Gulch, we reach Missouri City, which is located on Missouri Flat at the foot of Quartz Hill and is quite an imposing village in appearance, there being many good buildings erected —principally frame with now and then a log and canvas one, besides innumerable tents.

At the time we reached there, these places were swarming with people, and business was active. Following through Missouri City, down Excelsior Gulch, we reach Russel's Gulch, which is well inhabited and is generally well worked; but at the time we were there, not one in ten of the claims were being worked because of the want of sufficient water; and this was the case in many other gulches, especially Lake Gulch. But before leaving, the ditch bringing water from Clear Creek around the mountains was opened, and the difficulty remedied.

In looking through the towns that border the various gulches, one is often amused, for there is that awkward and unsettled appearance pervading them, so characteristic of a new place. Here you will notice a two story, unpainted, hastily-put-up frame building and beside it, a low, squatty log enclosure with two apertures in it answering for a door and window, and frequently covered with a tent cloth for roofing or with boughs and earth. Frequently too, we see a half dozen additions that have been put up to meet the wants of the increasing family. And many of the signs that we see stuck up around the establishments (telling of the variety of occupations carried on within, and what is offered for sale) are literary curiosities. One establishment I remember seeing, constructed of three small tents, each of which was different in form and size, was the abode of a number of artists, besides being occupied as a saloon (for drinking and gambling), store, boot and shoe shop, barber shop, bakery, etc. In the background were two tables, on each of which was a pack of cards; then on one side was a tray of pies, cakes and bread, and on the other side a barber's chair; while at the entrance hung several pair of boots, moccasins, mittens, etc., together with several signs, one of which read "milk for sale." This establishment was undoubtedly that of an enterprising Yankee, who was endeavoring to whittle out a fortune with his wits and not at the expense of muscle.

Letter XI

Spring Gulch runs nearly south and has been almost worked out; only a few companies were at work in it at the time we were there. Using a Georgia rocker, they were laboring to disadvantage owing to the scarcity of water. The water was being dipped by the pails full from a mud hole in the vicinity, thus supplying the rocker.

In Lake Gulch, which is a very long and crooked gulch and mainly taking a southeast course,

"Rockers" or "cradles" helped to speed up the amount of gravel that a prospector could wash looking for gold. Ingersoll, *Knocking Aroud the Rockies*.

work was about commencing, those having claims there being engaged in "stripping" and throwing out the pay dirt to have it in readiness for washing when the ditch was completed. At the head of this gulch is a small lake or pond from which it takes its name, and some were drawing their dirt there and washing it. This pond is now the reservoir of the ditch. At the lower end of the gulch are some ten steam quartz mills, one or more saw mills, and shingle machines. The settlement through this gulch bears the name of Yankee Town.

The works through Pleasant Valley, which is a continuation of Lake Gulch, were being prosecuted in a lively and energetic manner and presented the most active scene that I witnessed in the mountains. The log buildings erected throughout its length, and which were variously occupied as dwellings, saloons, markets, etc., were extremely filthy, more so than was apparent in any of the other mining districts; and what was not surprising, considering the uncleanliness of their abodes and the surrounding mud and water, it was the locality of much sickness, the endemic malady, mountain fever, prevailing to considerable extent. At the time we passed through, there were several persons lying dangerously ill with it, and one or two had died the day previous.

Eureka Gulch runs directly west and contains twelve quartz mills, which are operating successfully.

Nevada Gulch takes a southwest course and also contains a large number of mills. Some of the richest quartz lodes within the mountains are found within its vicinity, among which may be mentioned the Burroughs, Gardner, Cook County, Kansas, etc.

The mountains around these mining districts present a dreary and barren appearance, being covered with but little verdure, and the timber that once covered them being cut off, leaving a multitude of stumps. Owing to the scarcity of feed here and rather than pay the exorbitant price of ten cents per pound for hay, we drove our cattle off to a ranche some three miles distant, and there got them herded, paying one dollar and fifty cents per head a month. The hay brought into this market is hauled a distance of from thirty to sixty miles and was often sold at one hundred dollars per ton; but before we left, such large quantities of it were being brought in that we could have bought it for forty dollars.

Quartz mining is now becoming the principal system carried forward in the Gregory and Russel districts, and it is the one on which the success of the country depends; hundreds of lodes, or "leads" as they were termed, having been discovered and opened the past season, and many of them have proved rich and valuable. In prospecting for these quartz veins, men are governed by what is termed the "blossom," which is seen cropping out here and there and indicating the presence of a crevice or lode. These crevices of quartz rock vary in width, being from one inch to several feet wide and bounded on either side by a wall of granite through which the quartz has been forced by the action of intense and continued heat. The quartz is of various density and color, but the majority of it is porous, presenting a honey comb appearance, their cavities being many times filled with iron pyrites; and we often find attached to the denser varieties, pieces of crystallized quartz or rock crystal, being crystallized in the form of prisms and six-sided pyramids, some perfectly colorless and white, while others are more opaque and frequently colored with iron. They often consist of pure silica and bear the name of Rocky Mountain diamonds. Some portions of quartz bear the indubitable marks of having been fused and are molded in various shapes. The color of the quartz is various, sometimes red but more often bearing the various shades of brown, and it is frequently white, being light and spongy in consistence.

These quartz veins run in various directions through the mountains, but the richest of them run nearly east and west. Those running in the other directions are less rich and appear to be of a posterior date, for they often intersect the others. The extent in which these veins may be pursued is various – they may run out at the depth of a few feet, or they may run out so deep that they cannot be prudently pursued. When they taper and are closed up by the wall rock, it is said that by blasting through it, the crevice again opens to its normal width and can again be pursued, but how much truth there is in this speculation, I am unable to say.

After a crevice is discovered, the miner proceeds to open the claim by sinking a shaft or hole into it, which is effected by blasting and the pick and shovel; and, as soon as needed, a windlass is erected over the shaft in order to draw up the pay dirt and quartz. Or the miner may commence his work by tunneling into the base of the mountain, thus reaching the vein and working it from beneath. After a sufficient quantity of quartz has been quarried out, it is taken to the mills, and there either crushed on shares or at so much per cord.

As I have before mentioned, hundreds of these quartz lodes have thus been opened in the sides and summits of the mountains, and every miner within the mountains has one or more of these claims, which they consider equal to so much "bank stock." But are all of these quartz veins profitable? By no means— many of them are worthless, good for nothing; and many a man has been ruined in his efforts to develop his claim, not receiving enough from his quartz to pay current expenses. It is said, and with truth I think, that not one in ten of the lodes discovered will pay. But there are others that are rich and valuable and are paying largely; among them may be mentioned the Gregory

This arrastra worked on the same principal that had been used for years, but instead of a horse pulling the stone around, this operation in Clear Creek used water power. Matthews, *Pencil Sketches of Colorado*.

Letter XI

lode, the Bobtail, Foote & Simmonds's, Mammoth, Grinnell, Topeka, Clay County, etc.

Quartz mining, like the other branches of mining, has its uncertainties, and much time, labor and money is often expended to no purpose. I have known men to go to work, sinking a shaft into their claim and carrying it down for a distance of twenty-five and thirty feet, hauling up the quartz and piling it away, waiting for an opportunity to get it crushed, considering that they had a "nice thing," and speculating on its yield of gold, their calculations based on the various prospects they had now and then obtained in washing the pay dirt; but on taking it to the mill, what was their dismay to learn that their rich quartz would not pay ten dollars to the cord—not enough, within sixty dollars, to pay for the crushing. And then the fault was charged to the mill; they could not consider that the quartz was deficient in gold, and would not believe it, until they had given another mill a trial, which turned out a like result. They then abandoned work and turned their attention to find a customer to buy, and at length found one, who had just come in, having a good team of mules. By a little skillful maneuvering, an exchange was affected; and the party who had now the means of getting out of the country started for the States before their dupe could make any new developments.

The quartz mills in the mountains number over 200, and the majority of them have been brought in and put up the past season. They are principally distributed through the gulches in Gregory and Russel districts, and twenty-five are located at Gold Hill in the Boulder district. It is not my object to specify these different mills or their location but merely to convey some idea of their *modus operandi*.

At the time we were in the quartz mining district, the prevailing opinion was that they were a failure; and this idea was strengthened and seemed plausible from the fact that those in operation, at least the major part of them, did not fulfill all that was required of them. The principal charge was true to some extent, and for three reasons—first, the quartz was not reduced as fine as it should have been, the stamps not being sufficiently heavy and not falling with sufficient force; second, the apparatus for amalgamating and collecting the gold was imperfect; and third, those operating the mills did not fully comprehend or understand their business.

The mills that were brought to the mountains are of varied size and make—some running four and six, others nine and twelve stamps, and they were brought in by as great a variety of men—some being attended by men of scientific attainments; others, by men of intelligence and good sense, who had had experience in mining; while others were attended and were to be operated by men who could not justly lay claim to any of the above requisitions; but none were attended with more than sufficient capital to set them up in running order, which is one cause of the delay of their successful operation.

The fact of there being rich gold bearing quartz in the mountains, is, I think, fully established; and the only question now is, are the mills adapted to the work? And will they provide for the successful working of the quartz?

The mills, thus far, have not been competent for the work, but that they will eventually be successful is beyond a reasonable doubt; for experience and experiments are suggesting and applying the needed improvements, both as regards defective machinery and defective operators.

Many of the mills have been badly located, having been erected in poor mining districts and at places where they could not

Letter XI

This was just one of several quartz mills in Gregory Gulch, which were used to grind and separate the rich ore from barren rock. It was an important but expensive process.
Frank Leslie's Illustrated Newspaper.

control a proper supply of water, being compelled to remain idle for days and weeks on this account, and many of them are poorly set up and badly constructed. The mills most favored, and which are considered best, are those manufactured by Gates & Co. of Chicago, and of which there are a large number in the mountains.

When a mill is brought in, the proprietors hunt for a location, and when found they proceed to cutting the timbers for the frame, to the construction of a reservoir and cistern, and to the erection of a covering for the mill and a suitable abode for themselves and their company. When this is accomplished, they are ready for operation. But the miners look with suspicion upon many of these mills, and the mill men generally have to wait some little time until they can secure the acquaintance and confidence of their distrustful neighbors, unless they have claims of their own on which they can proceed to work, as many of them have or soon secure. Sometimes this is without any effort on their part; for there are many men within the mountains who make it a business to prospect quartz lodes and will stake you off a claim and get it recorded for the small consideration of a dollar or two, and which they will warrant to be the "genuine thing" and in a rich district.

The majority of the mills work but six stamps; and a few are working arastras in connection with them, which assist in pulverizing the quartz, acting upon it after it leaves the stamps, and they are, in the opinion of many, a great acquisition, facilitating the separation and hence the saving of the gold. A good mill will crush from three to four cords of quartz in twenty-four hours, which will weigh from eighteen to twenty tons. The usual charge for crushing is half the gold taken out of the quartz; but more generally, and especially if the quartz has no fixed or determined value, it is done at regular rates, varying from fifty to seventy-five dollars per cord.

The gold contained in the quartz is very fine and seldom visible to the naked eye, even in the richest specimens. The means employed for saving and collecting it is quicksilver, which is either spread over the surface of sheet copper or placed in pools or puddles along the sluice. As the gold passes over it, the two easily combine, forming an amalgam from which the gold is readily separated by a process called retorting—the mercury being driven off by heat, leaving the gold behind.

A large proportion of the quicksilver that has been carried to the mountain and used in the collection of gold has been an impure article; and we may state this to be one of the drawbacks to the successful operating of the mills. Its waste in using is stated to be about twenty-five percent.

Letter XI

Speculation in claims is carried on to a large extent, and it was almost impossible to get a claim, especially in the gulches or in the new "patch diggings" on Quartz Hill. Speculators would get hold of them and hold them, working them once in ten days to keep the title good, and the balance of the time engaged in looking up customers to sell to. Thus the majority of the claims in the mining districts are held, and though hundreds of them were idle and scarcely opened, it was impossible for a person to get one without paying their full value, which was always over estimated by their owner. I have known persons within the mountains who were holding from ten to fifty claims; and provided you wished to get one, the terms of purchase were so much cash down—generally from one-third to one-half of the valuation—and the balance to be paid in weekly installments or as fast as it was taken from the claim. But few of the men who went to the mountains the past year were able or felt disposed to purchase at these rates, and on finding the ground all taken up and no chance for securing a paying claim, would start for some other locality or go back to the States.

Quartz Hill, where are located the newly discovered "patch diggings," is situated between Missouri City and Nevada Gulch. At the time we reached there, mining operations, which had been delayed for the want of water, were about commencing, and the whole surface of the hill presented a most active scene. Hundreds of men were busy in excavating and throwing up the pay dirt, building and locating sluices and habitations, and digging channels from the consolidated ditch for a supply of water. Every foot of ground had been staked off and claimed, and a high price wanted for those in the most remote and poor situations. Some few nuggets had been found over the surface of the hill, one of which was discovered on a house-top, where it had been thrown with the dirt, and worth nearly fifty dollars. It was discovered by the owner of the house while engaged in sweeping the hail from the roof, which had fallen the preceding night. Some few of the claims in this locality were paying as high as $200 dollars per day, but the majority being worked were not so profitable, some even did not pay fifty cents per day to the man. We prospected in several claims and failed in raising more than a small color in claims that were reputed to be worth a thousand dollars and could not be bought for less. There are several rich quartz lodes running through this hill, in various directions, and which are being worked successfully. One of them, known as the "Ingles lead," has the widest crevice of any vein that I saw opened within the mountains.

Salting claims is carried on to some extent by "sharpers," and especially by those "who are soon going back to the States;" who have recently heard, as they relate, of "important business" or of the "sickness of their families—good claim—wouldn't sell, if were not obliged to—under the circumstances, sell cheap." Thus they talk to a customer, who of course inquires into the richness of the claim, which the proprietor proceeds to develop in a most satisfactory manner, and if a man is so blind that he fails to detect the cheat, a sale is generally affected.

In proceeding up the hill one morning, my attention was directed to a man who was busily engaged in salting a claim located on its side, and I stopped to notice the operation, concealing myself behind a pine in the vicinity. He had dug a small trench in the corners of the claim, and taking from his pocket a small package of dust, emptied it into his pan, mixed it up with a small portion of dirt, and some of which was then scattered along each trench. The operation was completed with the exception of filling up the trenches, which he was proceeding to do, when I hailed him, asking what he asked for the claim. He turned and eyed me for a minute, seemingly astonished to find anyone in so close proximity.

"An' d'ye want to buy?" said he, with an accent that told of his home in "Ould Ireland," and his education in America.

"Of course I want to buy, if you'll warrant the claim to contain more gold than you just now put in," said I.

"Whist, now! An' ye's was afther knowin' to the thrick was ye?"

I told him that I could not well avoid seeing him and asked him his purpose. He said that he had been "chated" in the claim, and was "afther" getting his money back. His price was twenty-five dollars.

We were very pleasantly located at the head of Lake Gulch and generally had plenty of company, there being several encampments besides our own, and in the vicinity was a settlement of miners engaged in quartz mining on the hill side around. From our position, we could look over into Nevada and Spring Gulches, having a fine view of Quartz Hill, and further back we could see several of the tall peaks of the snowy range; and we were within hearing of the rattle and jar of the mills, which kept up a steady stamping night and day, and the click, click of the drills, deep down in the mines, preparing for the blasts, which now and then resounded from every quarter, often filling the air with flying fragments of rock; and then the shrill screaming of the steam whistles often awaken the echoes of the mountains, carrying our thoughts back to the far off home. It was a strange sound to be heard within the wilds of the mountains; yet it was a cheerful one—telling of enterprise and progress and proclaiming that here would be the seat of a populous and powerful community in the future.

Emigrants were arriving and departing daily, but the departures were in the ascendant—the stampede back to the States was carried on briskly. Now and then a prospecting party was seen coming in, who had been out looking up "diggings," each with a pack on his back, a gun on his shoulder, and with a wearied and woe-begone aspect that reflected disappointment in every motion and every feature. Occasionally a miner who was changing his quarters might be seen driving a Spanish Jack loaded with his tools and grub and singing "A Few Days," keeping time with a baton, which was applied to the rump of the animal with "full measure" at every step.

Every day or so, we started out on a prospecting tour, digging into the mountain sides and delving into the gulches; and we have thus turned up many quantities of earth and stone, but little gold; and we always left our prospect holes with the consoling idea (which our friends often suggested) that we didn't go deep enough. When returning to our camp at night, we would gather together a large pile of pine boughs and build a roaring fire, when our neighbors would call around, and jokes, stories, and "experience" would circulate, illuminating what the heavy fire failed to do until bedtime, when each would crawl away to his "kennel" to dream of better accommodations.

Fires among the pine forests of surrounding mountains were quite frequent, and the heavy flames might be seen rolling, leaping, and breaking in huge columns above and around us and the smoke emitted being so dense and heavy as to darken the sun. Many, in passing over the mountains, have been caught, hemmed in with a furious belt of fire, and there being no escape, have perished. The charred skeletons of cattle and horses are often noticed that have perished in this manner.

We frequently saw our old friends with whom we had traversed the plains. They were located in Russel Gulch and were setting up their mill, having secured a good site, and were using all possible expediency getting it ready for operation. Some of the members of the company were securing "mountain stock" in the shape of quartz lodes as fast as possible, expecting a big dividend next year. Russel's Gulch had generally paid well; the claims paying ten and fifteen dollars per day to the man. There are several gulches leading out of it—the Graham, Leavenworth, etc.—and which are considered rich gulches.

In our daily search through the various mining districts, we often met with many pleasant incidents and sometimes saw strange sights. Passing over the Missouri Flat one day, we noticed a trio of Africa's sunny children digging for "golden sand," and they were working with such good cheer and heart that we felt disposed to stop and inquire into their business; so we asked how they were doing, and the sluice feeder very politely informed us that they were "making grub, sah." They informed us that they were direct from Georgia and had had some "'sperience" in mining, but "day did not like de country, and 'spected for to go back sum time in de fall." Hoping that they might make a nice thing before "dey leff," we passed on.

In our track, we found a party of miners sitting around their claim chatting and occasionally scratching, which later especially called our attention, and we noticed them more closely; one of them particularly was constantly digging most vigorously and had his efforts been directed in his claim, the result would have been different. At every bite he would reach for the invader and at times was victor, bringing out a big louse about the size of a grain of wheat and casting it away, while he kept on talking, having doubtless become so accustomed that the matter "passed him by as the idle wind, which he respected not" except when the animals started out to feed. The sight was one calculated to disturb a healthy stomach, to say nothing of various perverted nervous sensations that are apt to occur at such a spectacle; yet it was one extremely common in the mountains for the reason that men pay so little attention to personal cleanliness, going from week to week without ablution or changing their clothes, which they continually wear, both day and night, sometimes until they drop from them; and it can but be expected that this horrid species of vermin will take advantage of the neglect and carelessness of many. When they are once installed, it is almost impossible to rid of them, and it can only be done by burning the garments in which they are habited. They multiply fast, and if means are not taken to destroy them and their nits, they soon overrun the body, many times eating and burrowing under the skin and producing excruciating suffering.

LETTER XII

RAINY SEASON—HOW OLD MINERS REGARD NEW ONES—FAMILY QUARREL—THE DIFFERENT MINING REGIONS—START FOR BOULDER CITY, AND REACH IT—MEET A PIONEER, AND LEARN SOMETHING—PRICES OF PROVISIONS—START FOR AMERICA—TROUT FISHING—ST. VRAIN'S FORT—THE VALEDICTORY.

The rainy season commences about the first of July and continues nearly two months, rain falling every day but not continuously; occurring generally every afternoon in a succession of showers, which are invariably accompanied by heavy thunder and lightning that is terrifying; the thunder being almost constant—now and then booming like heavy artillery above us and rolling from peak to peak in ceaseless reverberations, while the swift and burning lightning illumes the misty mountain tops and the somber gorges, now and then descending with a crash amid the timber. The rain falls in torrents, coming in thick, heavy drops, and is often succeeded by a shower of hail, which is very destructive.

The climate of the mountains is generally mild and agreeable. The weather during the summer season, warm and pleasant; but the temperature of the nights and early mornings are rather too cool for comfort, especially in the vicinity of the "dividing ridge," where we find the eternal snow covering the summit. But as we approach nearer to the plains, the temperature rises, and we do not experience any very essential difference between it and the climates to that of Mexico, being hot and sultry, and currents of hot air continually circulating, parching and blasting all vegetation—a drought generally prevailing—and nothing will grow or flourish, except where irrigation is employed. The seasons in the mountains are short, there being but a short time intervening between snow and snow, which usually commences to fall about the first of September and continues until April. The climate is very different from that of California; which is so remarkable in its periodic changes and for its wet and dry seasons that divide the year into about equal parts; and which is well adapted for the purposes of agriculture and luxuriant growth of vegetation.

I frequently saw attempts at gardening within the mountains; but it was only in the valleys of the streams that it was successfully carried forward, and even there, vegetables did not properly mature. In one garden that I saw about the first of August, the sprouts of the various vegetables were scarcely above ground, although the seed had been sown a month or more previous—everything looked dwarfish and sickly. The gardens, however, at Golden City and in the vicinity of Boulder, which are well attended and watered, looked more thrifty and were more profitable, their various products being in good demand and bringing large prices.

In traversing the mountains, one cannot fail to notice the peculiar feeling that is evinced by resident miners towards those who are making their first debut into the mountains, which arises in part from the promptings of an avaricious spirit and from a natural jealousy of disposition. They generally know all the particulars relating to the country, its richness, prospects, etc., and consider the majority of "freshmen" a set of "damphools" and treat them accordingly. If you ask them how they are doing, some will preserve a dignified silence,

Letter XII

while others will perhaps convey the ambiguous answer that they are "making grub." If you wish to find out whether there are any vacant claims in the district, their answer is a decided negative—"they don't know of any" – when perhaps there are several, and unless you are sharp enough to make them point out their corners, you will never find out. They laugh and look wise if you condemn the country, and indirectly call you lazy when you tell of your failures. They speak of Stampeders as of no good to the country "ennyhow" if they did remain and were glad to get rid of them. If you should express yourself pleased with the country and calculated to remain in it, they unbend a little and are communicative; and provided you locate in the district, they perhaps know of some claim that can be "jumped" and will offer to stand by you in case of trouble. They eventually become quite sociable; but yet they require that they shall be considered "cock of the walk," and because they "come first," they are, of course, entitled to respect, and importance must be attached to their opinions.

One evening, while we were engaged in cooking our supper, our attention was called to notice a family, consisting of man, wife and nine children, besides a boarder, who had that afternoon pitched their tent within a short distance of our own, by hearing a loud and angry discussion between the woman and one of her sons, and in which the whole family seemed to be interested. Our curiosity was excited, and as the matter was assuming a tragic character, we postponed our culinary operations and turned from our "fry" to look upon a domestic "broil," and we beheld a large, willful, overgrown boy of eighteen years hurling stones and swearing at his infirm and aged mother. From among the debris of a fierce and angry altercation, we gathered these facts:

The family had just come in from Denver, where they had been keeping a public house, but which didn't pay, and as the sons and daughter wanted to get into the mountains, they had started for Gregory's. After encamping, the young man before mentioned wanting to proceed down into town, and considering that his linen was too dirty to be presentable, asked his mother for a shirt. She told him that he could not have one until Sunday, as she could not be continually washing shirts for him to change every few days. This naturally provoked the boy's spirit, and he commenced to curse and call his mother names (that would not look well if repeated here) and began to flourish his fists in the old lady's face, and she proceeded to correct him. Slaps were exchanged on both sides, and finally the boy commenced flinging chips and stones. The mother retreated, calling upon the father, who was standing at the mouth of the tent, a careless and apathetic spectator, to chastise him. He told her to get under cover and mind her business and that if the boy wanted a shirt, "why in h_ll didn't she give him one?"

"Mr. M_____," she said, "will you stand by thus indifferently and see a boy abuse his mother in this matter? Shame on you! You don't deserve the name of man, brute that you are. I will not put up with it!" And she proceeded towards the boy again, who had armed himself with a big stick and threatened, if she came near him, to knock her brains out.

An elder son then came forward, taking sides with his mother, telling his brother to put down the stick or he would make him. "Make me? Better try it on!" and stripping off their coats, they were about to engage, when the old man, the boarder, and the daughter rushed in to prevent the conflict, and the combatants were separated, but each breathing vengeance and hot with passion. By this time, the miners in the vicinity had collected around to the number of eight or ten, and the "happy family" went in under cover of the tent. But matters were not settled, for the jingle of words continued. Soon the girl came running

Letter XII

out into the road crying and the mother after her, telling her to come back.

"I won't come back, to be pounded by you. I'll die first!"

The boarder, who, it seems, was the girl's lover, then interfered, and taking the girl aside, began to talk to her; and the subject of the conversation was soon apparent, for the girl proceeded to get her things and was preparing to go off. This action the old lady objected to.

"What! Going away are you, with that shiftless, good-for-nothing fellow? Who will ruin you!"

"I will marry her," spoke the boarder.

"How will you support her? Here without money and without work."

"Shut up!" claimed the old man –"you ought to be hung!

"Oh yes, you would murder me, as you have tried to many times before. You are none too good to do it. Mr. M."—and the woman burst into tears.

"I will go, homeless, helpless and sick as I am—I can go and die." She proceeded to put on her bonnet and shawl and began to pick up what clothing she had.

"I do not want much—I will leave it for the children. I have toiled and worked hard for the past twenty-five years to bring up this large family, and then, at my age, to be brought from my home, dragged across the plains into this wilderness, and, after all, to be abused and threatened in this manner. It's too bad! Too bad!"

This appeal fell upon stony hearts, excepting those beating within the breasts of the spectators, who were standing partially concealed behind a miner's cabin near by, but it was not thought wise to interfere. The mother continued gathering up a parcel of clothes—more or less objection being made to her taking certain articles of apparel—and again a war of words ensued, the woman speaking in a high key, determined that we should all hear, while the man's voice was more subdued and was continually admonishing her to be more quiet and not show her character to everybody.

"My character is without reproach, sir, and I'm not afraid that the whole world should know it. It is you, sir, that's afraid to have yours known, which was bad enough at home—running away to cheat your neighbors, as you did. Oh, you good-for-nothing coward, you. You'll whip me, will you?"

"You're a liar!" spoke the man.

"You can call me a liar, and anything else, knowing that I am powerless to resent it, but you dare not come out and tell a man he lies, you poor, sneaking coward. I should think you'd be afraid to show your face to honest folks—crawling into the tent like a puppy."

Matters thus progressed—the woman alternately crying and scolding; and, as darkness settled over the scene, the war became more general. The girl was about leaving, being aided by the father, persuaded by the lover, and encouraged by the dutiful son, who, together with a younger brother, were packing up to accompany the sister. The mother's efforts were unavailing, and she came out and appealed to the group of miners, requesting their interference. We all proceeded into their camp and commenced an investigation, and learning that the boarder had been the prime instigator of all the trouble, judgment was passed upon him for creating mischief in the family, disturbing the peace of the community, and plotting the ruin of the girl; and the sentence of banishment was pronounced –ten minutes

Letter XII

time being given him to leave the district and if found after the expiration of that time, he could choose between twenty lashes and being hauled through the lake near by. The girl, who was only fourteen years of age, was then reasoned with on the impropriety of her conduct and told that she must remain with her mother. The father was also approached by several of the elder men and talked with concerning his conduct in the affair. He took the matter kindly and urged, in excuse, that "his wife had been unreasonable;" that he considered the boy as old enough to take care of himself and too old to be flogged; and, as for the girl, if "she loved the fellow, he didn't see why she might not go with him—he didn't care; he knew what his feelings were when he was young, and he wasn't going to control his children after they were old enough to judge for themselves."

"But you should exercise some government in your household if your children are too big to be corrected and especially strive to prevent such a scene as has lately been enacted. Many of us have children, but we warrant you, when they get so big that they cannot be corrected when they deserve it, we or they will have to leave, and the sooner the better. Your wife has been most shamefully treated, and by her own child, whom she has nursed and cherished and watched over for many long years; and now, when old, care-worn and sick, suffering in body and mind, to be so abused, is most shameful, sir! And you, her lawful protector, will sit by and see her brutally assaulted without the intervention of a word and pass the matter by without administering the punishment that the young scoundrel so richly merits. It does not speak well for the man, sir!"

Thus was the father talked with; and he finally admitted that he had been in the wrong to some extent. The time was nearly up that had been given the boarder to make "tracks," and he was again warned and told that his sentence would be carried out to the letter if he did not leave. He finally began to believe the matter no joke and, calling the girl aside, passed a few whispered words and started off; and that vicious son, who was his firm friend followed after. The mother pleaded with him to return, saying that she forgave him and telling him that he was not strong enough to start out into the mountains and care for himself. His reply was that he "didn't care a d__n, he was going to get out of her sight."

"You'll write to me and let me know where you are? Won't you, James?"

"Maybe!" was echoed back, and he was lost to sight in the darkness. The mother then told us that the boy had always been sickly, possessing a hemorrhagic condition of system, and at every little scratch, bleeding profusely; but we comforted her as best we could, telling her that the boy would soon repent and would soon tire of roughing it amid the mountains. Casting lots among the miners to see who should remain on watch during the night, for many expected that the scoundrels would come back and get the girl after all was quiet, we left the late scene of domestic strife, where—

All that the devil would do, if run stark mad,

Had been let loose—"

our pulses considerably accelerated with our efforts to restore harmony. The night passed in quiet, and in the morning the "amiable family" vacated the district; doubtless feeling that their little peculiarities and failings had been too freely exhibited to entitle them to respect, or make their society agreeable.

The gold bearing region of the Rocky Mountains, so far as discovered, extends from the North Fork of the Platte on the north, to the San Juan Mountains on the south, bearing off to the headwaters of the Blue and Arkansas Rivers and extending

Letter XII

The reports of some prospectors made it sound like every inch of dirt was a potential gold mine, but this drawing was a gross exaggeration. *Harper's Weekly.*

over to the Rio Colorado on the west, including the various diggings known as the Cache le Poudre, Boulder, Gregory's, Russel's, Clear Creek, Blue River, Arkansas, Buckskin Joe's, etc. A portion of these I have previously noticed and shall now refer briefly to the others.

Mining operations are carried forward on the borders of Clear Creek from the first range of the snowy axis to its confluence with the Platte River (South Fork), including the various localities known as Union District, Grass Valley Bar, Paine's Bar, Buckeye Bar, Spanish Bar, Chicago Bar, etc., all of which, with the exception of Union District, are being profitably worked. The gold found occurs in scales, pepitas, and, occasionally in nuggets.

The diggings at the head waters of the Blue in the vicinity of Tarryall have not generally met the expectations of the many who located there at the time of the discovery. Only a few claims there were rich and paid well, but the majority (and this is true in all of the mining districts) were unprofitable. A friend told me that he and four others took a claim in Hamilton District (No. 23) for which they paid $400, and after working it for a week, abandoned it, having obtained only thirty-five dollars, which was principally float gold; and their neighbors were generally as unsuccessful.

The mines at the headwaters of the Arkansas have been and still are profitably worked. A few of the claims in California Gulch have paid big, but the mines there are worked at considerable expense, there being a large amount of "stripping" to do before reaching the pay dirt.

Buckskin Joe's diggings take their name from the mountaineer who flourishes with that *soubriquet* (nickname), and who has been amid the mountains several years, having been a member of the Fremont rescue party. They were lately discovered and were said to be paying well.

The Boulder District is principally a quartz mining one, and its mines are located on and around what is known as Gold Hill, situated some twelve or fifteen miles back from the City of Boulder and some twenty or twenty-five miles north of Gregory's. Many lodes have been opened there, and many of them considered rich, but they have not, as yet, been sufficiently worked to test them, there being no mills there previous to June, 1860. A certain proportion of the lodes are doubtless rich, but the majority of them have not, as yet, and perhaps never will meet the anticipation of their owners. The quartz that has been crushed gives but a meager yield of gold—in some cases reported at $140 to $150 per cord, crushing three

Letter XII

cords of quartz, obtaining the very flattering result of about ten cents.

There has been 6,000 quartz lodes opened the past season in the mountains but one-third of them are not being worked for the want of capital; and capitalists in the mountains are said to be as scarce as mosquitoes in winter; and it is this need of money that delays the development of the country. The many who went to the mountains, and who are still remaining, are dependent on their daily labor for support, and if they obtain claims, as many of them do, they have no money to expend in their development. The price paid day laborers in Gregory is $2.50 and board. In California Gulch $3 and $3.50 are paid, which are the highest rates. If a man goes to work for another, he is not at all certain of his pay, for generally the men who employ have no means aside from their claims, and the employees must take risk with the employer. If the claim should prove valuable, they are paid; if not, they must wait and get it when they can. I have known several instances where poor men have been defrauded.

One instance in Lake Gulch, where a man advertised for laborers to work his claim, and he obtained several, and he set them to work (each man furnishing his own tools) stripping and throwing up the pay dirt in order to have it in readiness when the water was furnished. At the expiration of the week, pay was called for; but the proprietor was unable to meet their demands and stated as a reason that he had been disappointed in receiving what was due him from the Consolidated Ditch Company, but he should perhaps have it in a day or so. Thus days passed by, and finally Mr._____ was *non est inventus* (had not been found), and as another man laid claim to his effects, there was no method of securing their pay without dangerous trouble. Other and more aggravating instances might be cited. One man employed a large number of hands and kept them at work two weeks with "promises to pay" at the expiration of that time; but before the time had fully expired, he absconded with the proceeds of their labor. Search was being made for him at the time we were there.

Every mining district has its code of laws, and they all differ more or less, especially in the matter of holding and working claims. A man is generally entitled to three pre-emption claims, divided into a bar claim, gulch claim, and quartz lode, provided he opens the latter and works the two former once in ten days. By purchase he can hold as many as he pleases. The discoverer of new diggings is entitled to a "discovery claim" in addition to the one pre-empted; but discoverers are not generally satisfied with these and are apt to stake out as many of the most desirable as they wish, attaching a fictitious name to each—not only on the stakes but when sent in for record— he being, of course, the acting agent for the imaginary owners and at liberty to dispose of them as he pleases. The laws have of late been remodeled to some extent, I have learned; and claims, especially quartz lodes, are recognized as real estate, and persons can hold them whether they remain there or return to the States. The punishment of crimes is severe in all of the districts. Murder is punished with immediate death; and also theft, when the sum taken exceeds $100. When the sum taken is less, whipping and banishment is the penalty awarded.

The silver mines that have lately been discovered will doubtless open up another highway for the acquisition of wealth, if they prove as extensive and rich as has been represented and provided the means can be obtained for the successful working of them. These mines are principally located in the vicinity of the Blue River, the Arkansas, and in the vicinity of Gregory's in a locality situated back some twelve miles and called Silver Hill. I have seen various specimens of ore taken from the mines on the Blue that were decidedly rich; and it is said that the ore obtained from the various other mines is equally so; the assays made from it yielding ten and fifteen grains of pure silver to the ounce of ore. Rude smelts have already been erected in several localities and are doing comparatively well.

After remaining in the Gregory District sufficiently long to satisfy ourselves that everything there was "won by tricks," and considering that our chances for taking one with the hands we held looked rather dubious, and furthermore, knowing that it took a "flush" to play it alone, and we hadn't the papers, we determined to pass over to Boulder and see if we couldn't "make a point;" and "bidding" our friends there farewell, we started, proceeding via the Mount Vernon Road. We ascended the big hill with the help of one extra team of two yoke of cattle and encamped for the night in the valley of Beaver Creek, where we spent the following day in sporting. During the morning we started out to hunt rabbits and were quite successful, bringing several into camp at noon; and as we had seen trout in the stream, we devoted the afternoon in fishing for them, and the method adopted was to take a bag (after having fixed a hoop at the opened end) and place it in the stream, fill up the spaces on either side of it with stone, and then proceeding up the stream a considerable distance, commence thrashing the water with long whips, one on each bank until reaching the bag. We could not perform the business as it should have been done for the reason of the thick growth of bushes on either side, yet we considered that we could bag a few under the circumstances; but on reaching the bag and lifting it from the water, the exclamation of "nary one!" told our success; and though disappointed, yet not discouraged, we proceeded to try again, and with a like result. But remembering that

"Never give up, is the secret of glory,"

we ventured on one more trial, and by way of ensuring better success, we proceeded further up stream and instead of following the banks, waded down the creek and cut and slashed away in a most of-*fish*-ious manner, and as the bed of the stream was very rocky and slippery, we got occasionally what we were not looking for—a *duck*. We finally reached the bag, and proceeding along cautiously, one of the party took up the trap, and while we were waiting for the water to run out, we speculated on the number of trout we had. The water at last leaked out, and with it our luck—the bag was—empty, and we started back into camp with a very poor opinion of Rocky Mountain trout, and changing our dripping garments, we prepared our supper.

After regaling heartily on rabbit stew, we set fire to a large dry pine, and the flames were soon leaping and crackling far above us, shedding a flood of light through the valley, and

Clark reported that the towns of Denver and Auroria (shown here) had grown considerable, just during the short time that he was in the mountains.
New York Illustrated News.

lighting up the craggy mountains that encircled us. During the evening, we were startled by the rattle of spurs and the sound of approaching hoofs, and looking up, perceived a "solitary horseman" just emerging from the line of darkness into our brilliantly illuminated camp. He came near to where we were seated, dismounted, and throwing a steel shod pin into the earth, unfurled a lariat and staked out his horse with the exclamation, "There, Shellbark, go in!," then saluting us with "How are ye strangers?" squatted near us, asking "where ye from?" Giving him all the satisfaction we thought proper, he anticipated us in saying that he belonged over to Spring Valley Ranche, was herding cattle, and seeing the "big light tho't he'd come over and see what's up." Further inquiry revealed that he had been in the country five years; had been in the army as "bugler," had fought the Indians under Gen. Harney, had accompanied Col. Johnston to Salt Lake against the Mormons; and was twenty years old. He remained with us several hours, relating the incidents of his life—said there was only one thing that he loved in this world and that was "gambling and a little whiskey." Used to have great times at Salt Lake—won lots o' money—one time had his hat full of silver half dollars—couldn't keep 'em—money didn't do him no good—spent it fast as he got it." Said he "wouldn't go back to the States to live on no account, liked the mountains best, and was going to stay in 'em." He was a rude but jolly little fellow, and the evening passed very pleasantly, helping to fill up one of those monotonous blanks that so frequently attend the life of the traveler while passing through the solitudes of the mountains. But as our fire was dying out and a thick darkness was creeping over us, he pulled in his horse, and telling us that "Shellbark (his horse's name) could see his way home in the darkest night," mounted and rode off.

The next morning we resumed our journey, passing through lovely valleys and winding up and around towering mountains, their sides sometimes dark with forests of pine and sometimes with lofty precipices. Now and then we caught sight of a solitary windlass, indicating an open "lode," and surrounded with heaps of dirt and cords of quartz, which, in some instances, was being hauled to the mills. Occasionally we saw a parcel of men engaged in making shingles and shakes for market, cutting wood and prospecting, and now and then the buzz of the saw was heard, together with the puff, puff of the laboring steam as it escaped from work below, marking an era in the history of the mountains that had never before resounded with the sound of such industry that was cutting and shaving the heavy timber from their sides into "cradle bands" for the "rising generation," and into a commodity that brings sixty dollars per thousand in the cities and mining districts.

In the afternoon we reached the little village of Mount Vernon at the mouth of the canyon before described. It consists of a dozen or more buildings located on each side of the pass; one of which I noticed as being constructed of dressed stone that had been quarried in the vicinity. The mountain scenery in this locality is grand; the range running south is very broken and presents innumerable peaks, many of which are composed of limestone. Seen at the close of day, when the shadows are playing on them and the azure hues are creeping over them in the distance, with here and there the bright spots of golden light capping their pinnacles and streaming down their sides, they look magnificent and seem like a fairy creation, so light and fantastic are they in figure. The mountains rising up from the other side are more lofty, larger and less broken; and one of them presents a peculiar feature—three large pillars of granite pierce its summit and resemble the figures of three women—one standing, the other two kneeling—and so perfect was the resemblance that we were deluded into the belief that they were so in reality, until a passer-by, seeing that our attention was directed to them, told us what they were and added that

Letter XII

they might have been some of "Lot's family." The limestone in the vicinity is being quarried to a large extent, and several kilns have been erected for the burning of it.

Passing on we encamped beside the Denver City road, and the following day I proceeded to the city for letters and reached there at meridian, when I proceeded to Bradford's Corner, in which building is located the Post Office, P.P. & C. Express Co., and Hinckly's Express & Co.

Denver had improved wonderfully in appearance in the short time that had intervened since my last visit. Vacant lots had been filled up with good and comfortable buildings, and the streets were more regular; but business seemed less active; scarcely a team was to be seen in the streets, and all trade seemed to languish. The mint, which had been a late acquisition to the city, was in operation and had coined a large amount of the native gold—enough, it was said, to give to each person that had immigrated the sum of $6, if divided among them; but I rather think these figures are exaggerated. Various exchange offices were scattered throughout the city, the proprietors buying up

The Leavenworth and Pikes Peak Express Company carried important mail and supplies. Some of these men might be waiting for the actual arrival of a loved one on the stage. *Frank Leslie's Illustrated Newspaper.*

gold dust, for which they paid $14 per ounce for retorted or amalgamated gold, and $14.75 to $16 for scale and lump gold, which was well worth from $18 to $20; and in buying, they resort to base trickery many times, there being more than one "Shylock" among them. I was obliged to exchange some dust for coin in order to pay the postage on my letters and entered an exchange office for the purpose. Approaching the counter I exhibited a sample of my gold, which was a mixture of amalgamated and scale gold. The broker, after examining it, told me that it was worth $14.60 per ounce.

"No more?" said I.

"No, sir; that is all that it will bring, and all that I can afford to pay." And he stated that more "dust" was being offered him at those rates than he could find coin to pay for. I had expected at least $16 would have been offered for it, as it was passing currently among the miners for $17.50 and $18; but perceiving that I could do not better with him and not having time to "shop" around, I exchanged a sufficient amount to meet the demand at the Post Office.

In buying gold, they are very careful to extract all the dirt and black sand before weighing it. To affect this, it is subjected to several operations. First, it is placed in a mortar and broken, and after having been ground sufficiently, it is turned into a tin tray and subjected to the blowing process (which process they always prefer to perform behind the case, out of sight), which separates the dirt from it; after which the magnet is run through it, taking out the black sand, when it is weighed (and here, if you are not sharp, mistakes are often made); then the ounces, pennyweights and grains are counted and figured up, and you receive the value in coin.

Money was scarce in Denver and the other towns when we were there, and I have known twenty and twenty-five per cent to be paid per month for its use. Dust is the principal medium of circulation and is taken everywhere, except at the express office in payment for letters.

The P. P. & C. Express Co. had the exclusive control of the mails and charged exorbitant prices for the transportation of letters and paper—twenty five cents being demanded for every letter and paper delivered, and the same sum must be pre-paid on every one received. The office was continually besieged by the arriving emigrants—long strings being seen standing before the delivery windows, awaiting their turn at all hours of the day. Efforts have lately been made to affect some change in the postal arrangements; and the mails will, it is said, soon be carried through by government contract, which will revive a better state of feeling among the miners—many of whom have often rebelled against such extortionate demand, often threatening to subscribe to a fund for the establishment of an express company to carry their mail matter to the United States Post Office at O'Fallon's Bluff.

Horse stealing was being carried on extensively, and the day previous to my arrival one of a gang had been captured; but he told a plausible story of having been duped by the gang, who offered him the loan of one of the animals to ride back to the States. He had accepted, having been seeking some conveyance home for a long time. The judgment passed upon him was milder than it otherwise would have been, which was— punishment with the whip to the extent of thirty lashes. Murderous assaults and affrays were still common, and the lives of some of the best citizens had been threatened by the lawless bravadoes that infested the city; but of late, the city and surrounding country has been pretty thoroughly purged of them—some having been hung, others banished from the country.

After remaining in the city for a few hours, I started back for our encampment at the foot of the mountains. The day was excessively hot, but overtaking a load of hay that was proceeding into the mountains, I followed along under its shadow and at sunset reached my destination. But I was so fatigued with my journey of thirty long miles, and having suffered so much for the want of water, that I felt hardly *compos corpus* (able-bodied), and throwing myself down within the tent remained quiet until morning. During my travel in the morning I turned from the road many times, traveling along the banks and occasionally through the channel of a "dry run," where I frequently met with some fine specimens of petrifaction; the most remarkable of which was a portion of the cylinder of a tree having a diameter of about ten inches and a length of two feet.

The following day being the Sabbath, we remained in camp and spent a portion of the day in looking around a peculiar range of buttes running parallel with the mountains and rising up from twenty to one hundred feet in height. Along the ridge was a line of columnar basalt, looking like so much time-worn masonry, which here and there had crumbled away, strewing the slope on either side. At the distance of two miles back of us was a large, isolated, oval mountain, rising up some 1,200 to 1,500 feet above the level of the plain. This we visited and climbed to its summit, where we had one of the finest views that the eye can take in. Before us, and stretching out to the east till earth and sky were blended, lay the broad plain along which we could trace the sinuous windings of the Platte and its many tributaries by the timber that skirted their banks; to the left, lay a smooth, verdure clad-valley, skirted on the north by the Table Mountains with their broad and level summit surfaces and their rocky precipices, while resting at their feet reposed the quiet little town of Golden City with its many scattered buildings and snowy tents; and further on, and high above it, lay Golden Gate, peeping out from the mouth of the canyon; while yet further in the dim distance could be seen the rocky battlements of the mountains near Boulder; and back of us were the mighty monuments of ages—

> "*Amidst immensity they tower sublime,*
>
> *Winter's eternal palace, built by Time"—*

while to the right, another stretch of the plain met the eye, bearing on its bosom the prodigy of the mountains—the city of Denver.

Monday morning we resumed our journey, passing through Golden City, which was fast improving in appearance. Following along the base of the Table Mountains and finally emerging out upon the plain, our road led us across several small streams and over a high rolling plain.

There are three roads to Boulder; one follows along the base of the mountains, which is the nearest, and brings us to that town after traveling the distance of fifteen miles, but it is very rough and stony and seldom traveled with wagons. The next road takes us twenty-five miles before reaching it, and the other, thirty. We took the middle road and traveled across some lofty hills and ridges; encamping at noon on the bank of a very pretty stream, where we partook of lunch and then started on again but had not proceeded far before a heavy rain storm overtook us accompanied by a great deal of wind and thunder and lightning; but we had noticed its approach, as it came rolling over the mountains' tops, and were prepared for it. It soon passed over, but the roads remained muddy and slippery, the soil consisting of blue clay, and so plastic and adhesive had it become that the wagon wheels were soon encrusted with it. Our boots would gather pound after pound, rendering our progress slow and tiresome, and it was often difficult for the cattle to ascend the steep portions that were occasionally met with. In fact, they could make no progress in the beaten track, and we found it necessary to turn from the road and traverse over the turf. We had calculated on reaching Boulder at night, but darkness overtook us some ten miles this side, and we were obliged to encamp near a "dry run" through which the water had long forgot to flow. Cold Creek we knew to be in the vicinity, but all hope of reaching it was cut off by the increasing darkness, made blacker by the heavy storm clouds spreading around us. We were without water and consequently had to do without supper, but during the evening caught enough from the clouds for drinking purposes.

At break of day the following morning, we were again pursuing our course and reached, after an hour's travel, the banks of Cold Creek, where we concluded to remain the balance of the day, as one of our bullocks had during the night been "alkalized" from drinking bad water and was "scouring" profusely. Besides we had left our camp of the night previous forgetting a key of powder, which, as was our custom, had been taken from the wagon on the approach of the storm and hid away at a safe distance from the camp; and one of us had to proceed back after it. During the afternoon, while lazily seated under the shadow of the wagon, one of the party spotted near the mountains, what he considered to be a buffalo making for the creek at a slow "lope." Said he knew it was a buffalo by its make—its "high shoulders and tapering rump"—and in fact, the animal did appear to be a bison; and although it was distant some three miles, we decided to take after it, calculating that the animal would stop under the shade of the trees on the border of the stream.

We soon lost sight of our buffalo behind the timber but continued on, sometimes running and sometimes walking, for a distance of two miles, when my companion, considering that the sun was too hot and the game too uncertain for so long a jaunt, fell back, while I continued on. I had marked the spot where I had last seen the object of my pursuit and on nearing the vicinity proceeded more cautiously, creeping along under cover of the bushes, soon reaching a point opposite my aim, but there was no sign of a buffalo. Thinking that perhaps I might have been mistaken in the locality, I proceeded on and soon saw the encampment of some hay-makers, one of whom I questioned as to whether he had seen any game about, said he had not—"hadn't seen any since he had been there." I then told him that I had seen a buffalo in their vicinity, coming down from the bluffs to drink.

It was every man's dream to "Strike It Rich." Even if they weren't as knowledgeable and well-prepared as Clark, they hoped they might do it by accident. *Thayer.*

Says he, "I guess you have been slightly sold. We've got some cattle running around loose here, and one of them has been frisking about considerably this morning, and I rather think, stranger, if you'll look around that divide you'll see your buffalo—but don't shoot him!" Sure enough, my tramp of three miles through the broiling sun had resulted in a very provoking *sell*. Crossing the stream, I strolled leisurely back, meditating on the uncertainty of such sport, and thinking—

> "—At heart, with courtly Chesterfield,
>
> Who, after a long chase o'er hills, dale, bushes,
>
> And what not, though he rode beyond all price,
>
> Ask'd next day 'if men ever hunted twice?'"

I wisely concluded that I should not attempt the performance of any more such feats for the present—running the risk of being made the target for my companions to laugh at. But in this particular instance, they were about as deep in the mire as myself and "couldn't say much."

Proceeding back on the opposite bank from the one I had followed up, I soon found myself amid a den of snakes, who were laying stretched out at full length in the various paths to their holes, but they scattered about as soon as I did and descended into their slimy abodes; while I, giving them a wide berth, started into camp, not knowing which party had suffered more fright. Snakes were plentiful along the banks of the stream, and we frequently saw both rattle and bull snakes during the day, but having a constitutional fear of the whole race, we did not disturb them.

The following morning we proceeded to the accomplishment of our journey, and on rising the next ridge we had a fine view of Long's Peak and the valley of Boulder Creek; while far back to the south we could see the dim outline of Pike's Peak, which is the only peak of the mountains that the most people are acquainted with and which furnishes a title for the country. Before reaching Boulder we met with a large number of emigrants passing from there to the mines at Gregory's—some of them fresh from the States, while others had been engaged in the Boulder mines. Many of them stated that they were going to Mountain City to "look about," and doubtless they were going to wait, like Micawber (a Dicken's character who always was involved in "get rich quick" schemes) for "something to turn up," as the majority do, imagining that success in the mountains depends on luck, and to be sure it does to some extent; but it is that peculiar luck which is the *sequitur* (it follows "that") of energy and perseverance together with a vast amount of hard labor. If men go to the mountains with the idea that luck is going to point them to a fortune, or if they dream of hidden caves of treasure where big nuggets can be had for the lifting, I can assure them that a little travel through the mountains will seldom fail to regulate their imaginations, and they will begin to realize the fact that fortune is as fickle there as at home; and furthermore, that if they would but exercise the same ambition, the same study, and put forth the same labor on their farms or in their business at home that is necessary in the mines, they would have no occasion to look to "Pike's Peak" for wealth, or for the means to pay debts, and in the mean time could live much better and more happily.

A large proportion of the emigration last spring consisted of farmers, many of whose farms were encumbered with mortgages and taxes, and "Pike's Peak" opened up to their imaginations that means wherewith to cancel their obligations and free their property. I met many who were thus circumstanced, and they were all free to admit that had they remained at home, directed their attention to their farms, and saved the expense of their outfit that they should have been much better off, for now they were more deeply involved than ever, suffering hardship and privations, and barely receiving the wages given to the laborers in the States.

We finally reached the broad valley of Boulder Creek and encamped near the North Fork at a distance of a mile from the town for the purpose of securing good feed for our cattle. In the afternoon we proceeded into the city, following up the bank of the stream to the crossing, which consisted of a single pine log with a flat, hewn surface, each end resting upon a large block. The stream had a width of about thirty feet and had a strong current. We hesitated some moments before a sufficient confidence was established between mind and matter; but we had reason to believe that our head was straight and our feet firm, and we mounted to perform, *a la Blondin* (a French tight-rope walker), the feat of crossing a small Niagara. The log, having no central supports, began to spring and tremble as we approached the middle, and the whirling and rushing water below began to exercise a very disagreeable influence on my brain; but I kept on, expecting each moment that I should be compelled to sit down, for my balance began to waver and had the end not been near, I should have been obliged to have straddled the timber or have taken a dangerous fall; but I was fortunate in reaching *terra firma* without resorting to the humiliating position on the one hand or suffering the dire calamity on the other; and my companion was equally fortunate.

We soon reached the town of Boulder, which comprises some thirty log buildings arranged in a row on each side of the street; many of them occupied for stores and offices. The town seemed almost deserted at the time we entered it, and the only life apparent was seen at the lower end of town, where a small group of citizens were seated at the entrance of a saloon, engaged in whittling and talking over the future of the country. Some few tents were scattered through town; occupied by persons whose prone and supine positions indicate extreme laziness and an abundant nothing-to-do aspect, which in fact was a characteristic of the town, and I could not help contrasting its dullness with the life and activity of the other mountain cities. Many of the mountains in the vicinity are masses of bare rock, towering high above the plain and terminating in many irregular and jagged peaks whose outlines form many fantastic figures.

Letter XII

"*And all is rock at random thrown,*

Black waves, bare crags, and banks of stone"—

And in viewing them one cannot but wonder at what the poet calls—

"*—the astonishing magnificence of unintelligible creation,*" which is here displayed.

We remained in the vicinity of town several days, during which time we met with a Mr. A____, who was one of the pioneer miners, having reached this point in the spring of 1858 with a party of ten persons. He said, pointing to a copse of bushes near by, that there he had slept for many a night, rolled in his blanket, when the snow was two feet deep. In further conversation with him he gave us some account of his early experience in the country, which I give in nearly his own words, so far as memory serves me:

"On reaching the mountains, my companions and I commenced operations—prospecting and digging in various localities. We were often visited by parties of Indians. One day the head chief of the Arapahos came to us and said: 'What for you white men come here, dig our land, kill our game? Me expect present—my papoose hungry—want heap present, or me go to war' and said that he would give me three days to consider.

"I asked him, for I could speak their language to some extent having been with and among various tribes of Indians for several years, why he wished to go to war with us? We had never and did not intend to injure their land or property.

"He said: 'Does white man remember, many, many moons ago, of the great light in the west, when the stars fell? The Great Spirit told us then that white man would soon be as numerous as the falling stars and would overpower us; and the next day we saw the first white man that ever came into our country, and we must drive them out or make them feed us; and if you refuse to give us meat we must go to war.'

"He seemed to reason that the meteoric shower of 1833 foretold their destiny, and that they should try to avert it. We had been living in a tent but immediately after the old chief had declared his intention we set to work putting up a log house, and constructed it as firm and strong as possible and had it completed by the second day; but by-the-by, another party of five men, who had just arrived from the States, joined us, and expressed themselves as willing and determined to stand by to the last in defense of our rights. We were all well armed, had plenty of ammunition, and considered that our chances of victory were certain. The Indians were encamped some half mile from us; and on the eve of the third day the squaws had a pow-wow, and such horrid, unearthly cries and sounds, you never heard. The war-dance was also celebrated and far into the night we could hear the ta-too of their rude drums and the fierce yells of the braves, as they circled around their fires.

"We spent the night in preparation—forming plans and getting everything in readiness for the conflict on the morrow.

"This morning of the third day at length dawned, and my men all stood willing and ready; but where were our five friends who had agreed to stand by us? They were missing; but we little cared to have such cowards, as they had proved themselves, in our company; they would have done us more harm than good. The sun arose, but the Indian camp was still quiet, which we were all intently watching; but soon, and much to our surprise, the old chief was seen approaching, unattended by any of his tribe. I directed my men to conceal themselves; and in order to make it appear that we cared but little for his

Letter XII

threats, I went and unfastened the door and then lay down. The chief approached and knocked at the door. I told him to come in, and as he entered, I got up. He approached me, and folding his arms about me, gave me a very affectionate embrace, saying that the Great Spirit had told him to take pity on the little band of whites and not massacre them; and he said further that white man good friends now—live in peace—all of which was very gratifying to us; and the next day we killed one of our bullocks and invited the chief and his family to eat with us, while the balance of the ox was distributed among the tribe, and never in my life did I enjoy a feast equal to that with the Arapahoe chief.

"We never had any further trouble with them and but little with the other tribes. The Utes, a short time after, made a descent upon some settlers in our vicinity and badly wounded one woman and drove away several mules and several head of cattle; but they were so closely pursued by us that we recovered a large portion of it."

This is the sum and substance of the story told us by the pioneer, and which is doubtless true. He also informed us that he was the first man that took a genuine specimen of gold into Denver, and that he was the first discoverer of the mines at Gold Hill; and furthermore that he was now engaged with a company of men in turning the channel of the creek just above town and expected a large reward for their labors.

Provisions in the mountains have generally been plenty and have brought good prices. The miners have generally bought their supplies, whenever opportunity offered, from what they term, "Stampeders," and which they could often buy at low prices as compared with the market rates at Denver. Flour could be bought for $14 to $16 per hundred, and at times for $12 per hundred; corn meal for $7 and $10; beans, twelve and fifteen cents per pound; potatoes ten cents per pound (now selling for six dollars per bushel); butter sold at a price averaging from forty to sixty cents per pound; sugar, twenty-five and thirty cents per pound; coffee, twenty-five to fifty cents per pound; meat sold at twelve and fifteen cents per pound; milk, ten cents per quart; bacon sold for twenty and thirty cents per pound; and everything else in a like proportion. In affixing the price to the various articles for sale, ten cents was added per pound for transportation—this being the rate charged by the transportation companies.

We could not fix upon anything substantial on Boulder; and "Gold Hill," that obscure basis on which the people of Boulder have built their hopes, so fluctuated that the majority of our company considered that it was taking a big risk to have anything whatever to do with it, and as they were safely out of the mountains thought we had better keep out and start for America, where they might turn to some employment, which, if not so promising to the imagination, was more sure of yielding a livelihood. The motion was considered and the question put, and as the "Aye's" were in the ascendant, there was no other alternative for the "No's," than to prepare for the exodus. The following morning we turned our backs to the mountains, and with the fortune of experience that we had gathered, started for home, following down the St. Vrain road along the border of the creek and encamped early in the afternoon for the purpose of fishing, as we knew the stream to contain fine trout, having seen several anglers with a string of them pass during the afternoon. We had encamped near the junction of the North and South Branches of the stream, and just below a large butte, which rose up, isolated and alone, at a distance of seven miles from the mountains, and which the settlers had given the name of "Hog's Back."

Letter XII

The stream was wide, deep and swift, and its proportions eminently entitled to the appellation of river. Our hooks and lines were soon in proper trim and were thrown into the stream, and the sport commenced of lifting out some of the largest speckled trout that I ever saw, weighing from one to three pounds each. In half an hour's time we had hooked up a sufficient number to meet the demand, and they were served up in a style that would have gratified more capricious tastes than our own; and so exhilarating was the sport and so appetizing were the objects of it, that we remained in the locality the following day, devoting our time to fishing and to prospecting along the banks of the stream, and such was our success in the latter pastime that we quite earnestly considered the propriety of remaining to make further developments; but some of the party had fully made up their minds to leave the country and could not be induced to remain, and on the following morning we were again en route for home.

Passing on, we saw a large number of hay-makers at work, cutting and curing grass for the market in the mountains. The broad valley of the creek is very fertile and was generally well settled by a class of men who were turning their attention to agricultural pursuits, and the greater proportion of the whole valley, extending from Boulder to St. Vrain's, had been claimed and pre-emption shanties erected.

The road that we were traveling was a good level one and well provided with good grass and water, and I should judge it to be the best and most direct road to the mountains, being much nearer than the one via Denver.

The following day after leaving our fishing ground, we reached the Platte River, which is bridged at this point with a log structure that looked as though it would ill afford a safe transit, but we crossed very comfortably and found on the opposite bank, a toll house where they wanted six shilling for the damage done the bridge—we paid it, thanking fortune that it was the last toll operation that we had to pass through. Two miles further travel brought us to St. Vrain's Fort, where we stopped to rest for the day was very sultry and the air suffocating. The fort here has been used as a trading post with the Indians, but it is now in ruins; there are, however, two frame buildings erected here, one of which is still occupied by traders and is quite a rendezvous for Indians, but we saw none there at the time we passed by, as we were told that they had gone off into the Cache le Poudre country to hunt.

After leaving St. Vrain's, a distance of two miles brought us to the junction of the Denver City road, at which place a shoemaker had erected his tent and had displayed on a rough board in one corner, a row of black bottles containing, doubtless, a variety of whisky, from *proof* to *water-proof*. He was evidently on his *last pegs*, and, with his a(w)ll had located there, having been disappointed in his *findings* at the mountains, to raise the wind to get home, and for the want of boots to *sole*, he frequently *tapped* the bottles and *sold* the contents, which was decidedly the most profitable business.

We continued back, following along over the road, which no doubt the reader is sufficiently familiar with; and after thirty-five days of hard travel over the monotonous prairie, through rain and shine, heat and cold, and many times through the entire night for the purpose of escaping the torturous fangs of innumerable mosquitoes, and at times when the night was as dark as Erebus (Greek God of Darkness), and we could not see the length of our noses, when one of us would start ahead with the lantern in order that we might keep track, we finally reached our starting point of the Spring previous—having accomplished an over-land travel of some 1,500 miles in six months, behind the slow bullocks that had required about as much effort on our part as on theirs to keep them moving—feeling rich in experience, if not in money.

A large emigration is expected next Spring by those remaining in the mountains, and doubtless they will not be disappointed, for the country is fast being developed and settled; and as the mists of uncertainty that have hung over that country for the past two years are fast dissolving before the warming rays of a progressive and determined spirit, disclosing that substance of things hoped for—"that more than philosopher's stone"—the public confidence is being restored, and thousands will again prepare to try their fortune and their fate.

Quartz mining is to be the permanent feature of the region, and it is the only mining that will hold out and pay. The gulches and bars that have been discovered and worked have not generally paid, and they never will, unless means can be adopted to facilitate the working of them and to save the gold, much of which is very fine and wastes in the washing.

It is not at all probable that all who again start on the expedition will realize a tithe of their expectations, and for reasons that have been enumerated in the previous pages and for reasons that cannot but be apparent to every man who possesses common sense. All men are not successful in their avocations and experiments at home, and the laws that govern their finances and fortunes in the States will not be suspended in the mountains. If they are not suited for the business, and if they have not the means to carry it forward successfully, they will necessarily fail; and if they have not the courage to face difficulties, the ability for hard labor, and the perseverance and patience that is necessary, the probability is that they will be disappointed; and if any man goes there with the hope of making a fortune in one season, he will find himself mistaken, unless he is content with a very small one.

A large number went last spring without knowing exactly what they should do on reaching the mountains; and the majority of them left without finding out after standing around through the various mines with the hope of "jumping into somebody's shoes," for which there is seldom a chance. Capitalists can do well there, for they can turn their money in half the time that would be possible elsewhere; but the laboring man, who has but little means, or with scarcely enough to furnish a comfortable outfit, and who will be entirely dependent on his wits or muscle, had better remain at home, for he cannot get rich there any sooner than at home, and he will escape much hardship, toil and privation, which is necessarily entailed on those who sojourn amid the mountains. But it is not my purpose to either encourage or discourage any person. If a man thinks he can do well and wants to go—let him go—*"chacun a son goux"* (each according to his taste)!

The best route is, I think, the one that I have described; but perhaps the one from Omaha is the most direct and shortest, and it will eventually take precedence over all the others when the railroad is completed to that point. All persons intending to start for that country next spring should be at their starting point as early as the 20th of April and proceed out as soon as the feed will permit—the grass is generally far enough advanced at that time to afford good forage.

The outfit of companies would be too tedious to mention. Generally a light wagon—one sufficiently strong to convey 2,000 or 2,500 pounds—is the best vehicle; and, with regard to a team, cattle are best where you have much load to draw, and they are by far the most sure and safe and will not occasion one-half the anxiety and trouble that horses or mules do; but then the latter will perform the journey in one-half the time that is required where bullocks are used, as they will not travel to exceed an average of fifteen miles per day.

Letter XII

The best method to pursue in the matter of traveling is to get as early a start in the morning as possible—say four o'clock—and proceed until nine o'clock and halt until two o'clock p.m.; then resume and travel until six o'clock or until such time as may suit convenience. By pursuing this course, you will avoid the heat of the day, your team will travel faster and better, and they, as well as yourself, will reach the end of your trip in better condition than those who follow the old methodic system of reaching certain specified camps each night, where the feed is poor and perhaps all consumed by those who have preceded.

As regards the many other items that constitute a proper outfit, one will be governed by his own peculiarities or according to their taste and means. Everyone should be well supplied with waterproof clothing and with a sufficient quantity of blankets and bedding if they desire to pass the nights comfortably; the items of flour, meal, bacon, potatoes, molasses, sugar and coffee are the essentials; dried and preserved fruits, the condiments, and a good article of whisky are the (so considered) luxuries.

Every company should make it a point to take a cow, as she will more than pay for herself and the trouble during the trip and can be sold to good advantage after reaching the mountains.

The items of beans and bologna sausage should be left out. The first can never be properly cooked, especially while traveling, and will ever occasion more or less sickness when they are not properly prepared; the sausage, when eaten, creates great thirst, which cannot always be gratified, and even if it can be, the drinking of large quantities of water should be guarded against, as it weakens the system.

Finis

www.ingramcontent.com/pod-product-compliance
Lightning Source LLC
Chambersburg PA
CBHW061759110426
42742CB00012BB/2085